For Shelley Riley

Best wishes

Marjon Whitney

aug 23, 1979

CORNELIA
VANDERBILT
WHITNEY'S
DOLLHOUSE

CORNELIA VANDERBILT WHITNEY'S DOLLHOUSE

THE STORY OF A DOLLHOUSE AND THE PEOPLE WHO LIVED IN IT

MARYLOU WHITNEY

PHOTOGRAPHS BY E. MARTIN JESSEE

DRAWINGS BY JOUETT W. REDMON, JR.

FARRAR, STRAUS AND GIROUX

NEW YORK

Copyright © 1975 by Marylou Whitney

All rights reserved

Second printing, 1976

Printed in the United States of America

Published simultaneously in Canada by

McGraw-Hill Ryerson Ltd., Toronto

Designed by Cynthia Krupat

Library of Congress Cataloging in Publication Data

Whitney, Marylou.

Cornelia Vanderbilt Whitney's dollhouse.

1. Maple Hill, Ky. / 2. Kentucky—Biography.

3. Whitney family. / 4. Doll-houses. / I. Title.

F459.M35W47 1975 / 976.9'47 / 75-20080

AUTHOR'S NOTE

To write a completely accurate story of each family who lived at Maple Hill for the past one hundred and ninety years would be almost impossible, for I found only a few letters and no diaries. And often a story handed down from one generation to another has a little something added, a little something subtracted, in the telling. Consequently, some of the accounts may have been exaggerated and, perhaps, others may have been attributed to the wrong members of a family. Still, all the stories in this book are true ones. All dates are correct. Here and there I have imagined a conversation, or how a person must have felt in a certain situation. Based on what I learned about the people I write about here, I believe these little flights of fancy are permissible. For in the six years I spent researching my material, I feel I got to know these people well enough to take a few liberties with them so that you may see them more clearly.

Many people have helped me in the preparation of this book, and I welcome the opportunity to say thank you to Mrs. Emily Church, Sidney Combs, the Rev. Alfred M. Gormley, Mrs. Helen Johns, Mrs. H. A. Knorr, John W. Marr, Mrs. Benjamin Roach, J. R. Singer, Mrs. Kirkwood Snyder, Mrs. Samuel Walton, Mrs. Wade Hampton Whitley, and Mrs. Carl Wilson.

I would also like to express my special indebtedness to James A. Cogar, the well-known restoration expert and past president of the Shakertown, Kentucky, restoration project. It was my husband who put me on the path into the past of Maple Hill; it was Mr. Cogar's knowledgeable encouragement that kept me on it.

Early in the course of the research, I discovered that my rather mercurial temperament balked at reading seemingly endless issues of old newspapers. Here three of the children came to my rescue. Daughters Cornelia and Heather and son Hobbs cheerfully waded through reams of newsprint for me and supplied me with clear and useful notes.

Many books have helped me to understand the

historical background. Among the titles to which I have turned with some frequency are:

John James Audubon, *Delineations of American Scenery and Character,* reprint, New York, 1970; Thomas D. Clark, *Kentucky: Land of Contrast,* New York, 1968; Ermina Jett Darnell, *Folks of Elkhorn Church,* Louisville, Ky., 1946; Ruth H. Early, *The Family Early . . .* Lynchburg, Va., 1920; John Filson, *The Discovery and Settlement of Kentucky,* reprint, Ann Arbor, Mich., 1966; Charles H. Hamlin, *Virginia Ancestors and Adventures,* vol. 1, Baltimore, Md., 1974; Flora Gill Jacobs, *A History of Dolls' Houses,* New York, 1965; Kentucky State Historical Society, *Register,* vol. 34, no. 108, July 1936: "Joel Watkins' Diary of 1789," ed. by Virginia Smith Herold; Charles Kerr, ed., *History of Kentucky,* Chicago, 1922; Catherine Knorr, *Culpeper County, Virginia, Marriages,* 1907; Kyle McCormic, *The New-Kanawha River,* Charleston, W.Va., 1959; Clark McMeekin, *Old Kentucky Country,* New York, 1957; Museum of Science and Industry, *The Doll House of Colleen Moore,* Chicago, 1950; William Henry Perrin, ed., *History of Fayette County, Kentucky,* Chicago, 1882; George W. Ranck, *History of Lexington, Kentucky,* Cincinnati, 1872; Elizabeth M. Simpson, *Bluegrass Homes and Their*

Traditions, Lexington, 1932; William H. Townsend, *Lincoln and the Bluegrass,* Lexington, 1955; Frederick A. Virkus III, ed., *The Abridged Compendium of American Genealogy, First Families of America,* vol. 3, Chicago, 1928.

As I am not a trained historian, I cannot say too emphatically that none of the people who have been so generous with help is responsible for whatever errors may have crept into this account. They are my doing, and mine alone.

Marylou Whitney
Lexington, Kentucky
1975

CONTENTS

INTRODUCTION

3

THE ROGERS FAMILY

1784–1841

21

THE MUIRS

1841–1926

67

THE MARSHALLS, MCDOWELLS,

AND SANDUSKYS

1926–1951

91

THE KIRKPATRICKS, BENNETTS,

AND WHITNEYS

1951–1975

101

CORNELIA VANDERBILT WHITNEY'S

DOLLHOUSE

follows page 116

CORNELIA VANDERBILT WHITNEY'S DOLLHOUSE

INTRODUCTION

Seeing Cornelia's dollhouse for the first time after having just come from the main house can be, I'm told, a rather unsettling experience. It takes a moment or two to put everything, including yourself, into proper perspective. For inside this tiny house, an exact replica of the main house, is an exact replica of the very room you were sitting in a moment ago—right down to a gold filigree ashtray or Chinese bowl no bigger than an infant's fingernail!

When H.R.H. Princess Margaret and her husband, Lord Snowdon, visited us last year to attend the one hundredth running of the Kentucky Derby, she expressed an interest in seeing Cornelia's dollhouse, since Windsor Castle contains one of the world's most famous dollhouses. It was presented to her grandmother, Queen Mary, by her subjects.

So the princess grew up charmingly aware of the great beauty to be found in smallness. Seeing our dollhouse, she was especially intrigued with the miniature books in the library, each one a readable replica of a book to be found in the library in the main house. And she positively beamed at the sight of the handmade sterling-silver mint-julep cups filled with ice and mint and set on a silver tray on one of the terrace tables. Her Royal Highness had that very day tasted her first mint julep.

Everyone who sees Cornelia's dollhouse seems to have a favorite room, or piece of furniture, or *objet d'art*. It may be the hand-carved Chinese coral dog, one of the eighteenth-century chandeliers with over one thousand tiny crystals, or one of the many oil paintings hand-painted on very fine linen. It may be the Queen Anne tea table, the pine hutch cabinet topped with a conch shell and a basket of wild mustard, or the three-tiered table with snake feet that holds a Sheffield silver pitcher, a flower arrangement in a gold filigree pot, a Delft pitcher, and gold opera glasses. Others are enchanted with the gilt harp that has seven pedals and is actually positioned on E flat. Still others are fascinated by the pine coat rack holding a man's cane, and the real fern that lives on air and stands on an eight-

eenth-century drum table. And most women adore the tiny enameled ring box that opens to reveal a diamond ring inside.

I should imagine that there's something in the dollhouse to catch anyone's fancy. Just as the very thought of a dollhouse has always captured mine. And Cornelia's.

Cornelia already had several dollhouses when, at age nine, she confided to me that she'd like still another. *"Another* dollhouse?" my husband said when I told him. But I assured him that this one would be different. Not store-bought, but actually built from scratch by our workmen to be a replica of Maple Hill, the house on our horse farm in Kentucky. The place we consider our home and where we always spend our Christmas. I reminded Sonny that our workmen love it almost as much as we do and that they are capable of whittling the most beautiful, fragile objects imaginable. I further explained that such talented workmen as Ernest Hughes, Clarence Stacy, and Ray Edge didn't have enough to keep them busy on rainy and snowy days during the winter months. Just picture, I said, stately columns, exquisite paneling, all the little spokes in the staircases, done to dollhouse proportions by these artisans. And yes, the wood used to

build the dollhouse could be the old wood left over from the log cabins that first stood at the fort during the days of the Revolution, and later were used to build our house. Furthermore, Cornelia, the only native Kentuckian in our family, and I would plan the house with them, step by step. It would be a labor of love. And it would produce, I promised, a dollhouse worthy of a museum.

So, with my husband's permission, the project began. Jouett Redmon, our caretaker and an immensely talented artist, a descendant of the famous Kentucky artist, Matthew Jouett, did some preliminary sketches. And he agreed to supervise all the work. It was at this point that Sonny made a suggestion that was to give our project another, much broader dimension. He said that, since I was going to put so much time and money into this dollhouse, mightn't I like to trace the history of Maple Hill? After all, if we were going to create a dollhouse worthy of a museum, shouldn't we provide it with a family tree? To date, all we had was one tiny genealogical twig: the name of the family from whom Sonny had bought it in 1951.

I was delighted with his suggestion. I've always been a history buff, and I had long been curious about the people who had lived in our house. Now

The harp in the living room, tuned to E flat

here was a chance to satisfy my curiosity and learn something of Kentucky history in the process. But little did I know that first day I started off, with a small notebook in my hand, headed for the county courthouse to search for titles and deeds, that six years later I'd have bookcases full of research material.

With Cornelia at my elbow whenever her school schedule permitted, I zigzagged back and forth from the county courthouse to the Kentucky State Historical Society in Frankfort, our capital, to the state library there, and on to the basement of Duncan Tavern in Paris, Kentucky, restored by the Daughters of the American Revolution, and literally stuffed with important records and local memorabilia. And then, fed a clue here and a clue there, we began wandering through cemeteries and old burial grounds on private property, squinting down at ancient, weather-beaten gravestones. In fact, we began spending so much time in cemeteries that Cornelia and I started bringing our lunch and enjoying it under the trees, just as families used to do generations ago when a cemetery was practically a cultural center. Finally, with a tape recorder under my arm, I began the most entrancing part of my research: visits with descendants of the early occu-

pants of Maple Hill, or with old-timers in the area whose forebears had known them. And so, little by little, the story of our house began to write itself.

Meanwhile, Cornelia's dollhouse was shaping up, too. Each time I set off for a dental appointment in town, Jouett or one of the men working with him would ask me to "Please bring back any old tools they're not using." For the tiny tools that pick and poke and polish teeth were just the right size for some of the most delicate work being done in the dollhouse.

Sometimes, after a day spent poring over the handwritten records of Levi Todd, our first county clerk and the grandfather of Mary Todd Lincoln, I would come home and go directly to the carpenter shop on the farm where the dollhouse was being built. Often it didn't seem so much a dollhouse to me as a tiny piece of history. For now I knew something of the people who had lived in our house, who had given birth there and died there. And sometimes I thought that, had I known just a little of this history when I saw Maple Hill for the first time in 1958, I would have loved it on sight.

•

Sonny and I had been married only two weeks, and now he was introducing me to his beloved

Kentucky. Driving from the airport, he apologized for the fact that it was February. "It's the ugliest month here," he said, and from what I could see through the car window, which was at that moment being pelted with icy rain, he wasn't exaggerating. Although I had been born in Kansas City, I had spent years in Arizona and California, where sunshine is so constant that it's often a bore. But now when I peered through the windshield and saw only a sheet of ice on the road ahead, I thought how welcome even a sliver of sunshine would be. *This* was the legendary Bluegrass country?

As we turned off the road and passed between two enormous limestone entrance pillars, one of which carried an ice-covered sign reading C. V. WHITNEY FARM, Sonny's whole face seemed to brighten. And whenever that happens, my own dark mood lifts instantly. Now the icicles on the fences on either side of the road looked like so many rows of sparkling fringe. I said so, and Sonny laughed. As we turned off the main drive, the freezing rain seemed to let up and there was a most unexpected sight: a charming English cottage. Ivor Balding, the farm manager, and his wife, Frances, were at the door to greet us and show us to our rooms.

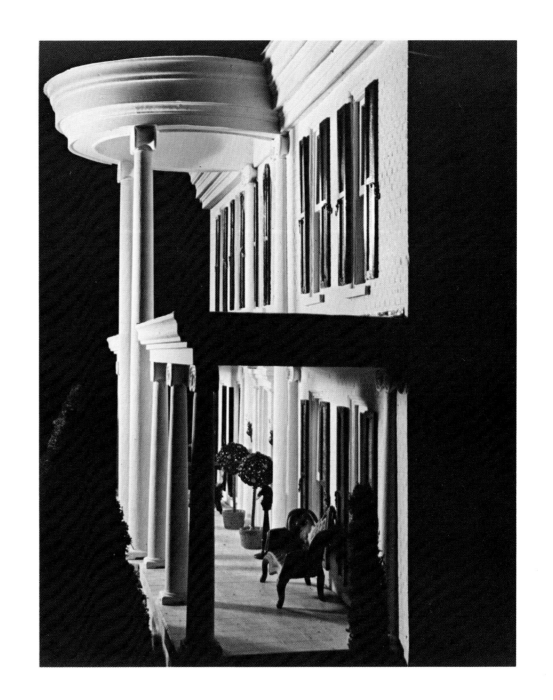

That evening we sat sipping our toddies before a lively fire. Sonny and Ivor discussed horses while I plied Frances with questions about the main house. All Sonny had told me about it was that he wanted it to be our home whenever we were in Kentucky, and that he hoped I would like it.

"Will I like it?" I asked Frances. Her answer was a noncommittal smile. Where was it located? She said it stood on a hill at the far end of the farm. Was it brick or frame? Brick. Were there pillars? What sort of windows did it have? I had a whole battery of questions, but she didn't really answer any more of them other than to say that she imagined it was quite an old house. "You'll see it to-morrow," she kept reminding me in a way that suggested she'd rather I see it and judge it for myself. Preparing for bed that night, I asked Sonny again about the house, but he replied that he was too tired to talk about it and, anyway, I would see it in the morning.

I awoke early the next morning to find the bedroom filled with winter sunlight. I literally ran to the window and there at last I saw the Bluegrass country I had expected to see: a rolling checkerboard of fenced meadows, with mares idly roaming the paddocks, their foals spindling along beside them.

A breakfast of country sausages, eggs, and hominy grits, and then Sonny and I were on our way to the house that no one seemed to want to tell me about. Much of the drive paralleled a meandering creek, and as we drove along under an arch of splendid oaks and sycamores, Sonny told me the story of its origins.

Once upon a time a beautiful Indian princess fell in love with a young brave. Unhappily, she was already betrothed to the brave's widowed father, the tribal chief. There was only one way out, and the young people took it. Hopping onto a giant elk named Wapiti, they eloped. Off they dashed one morning with the old chief in angry pursuit.

In the luxuriant valley where our farm now lies, he finally caught up with them. Arrows flew. One of them struck the elk. It was a mortal wound, but Wapiti was faithful to the end. Turning about in his death throes, he presented his mammoth horns, blocking the path of the chief long enough for the young lovers to escape. Then Wapiti fell dead; his horns sank into the ground and the creek sprang from them. It is called the Elkhorn, and it branches

*Maple Hill as it looked when I first saw it,
in 1958*

all over the fields, curving this way and that way, like the branching horns of an elk.

By the time Sonny finished his story, we had reached the front yard. I looked up and what I saw on top of the hill made me gasp. A dilapidated red brick farmhouse flanked by a tangle of chicken coops and pigsties, with most of their tenants scratching and rooting in the dank underbrush off the yard. Sonny's words echoed in my ears: "I want to start a new life with you here."

Here?

As we got out of the car and began walking toward the house, I remember wondering what in the world was holding up the porch roof; certainly not those thin and rotting posts. Sonny held my arm as we ascended the rickety steps. It was a gingerly trip on my part, but apparently not gingerly enough. I gave a shriek as one foot went through a worm-eaten floorboard. As I disengaged it and looked up at Sonny, I knew what he was thinking: I didn't like the place and he had so hoped I would.

"We could make some changes," he said rather tentatively. "Of course, that might take a little doing on your part."

Sonny knows how to influence me. I like a challenge, and this house was certainly a formidable one. I stepped back cautiously and looked up again at the façade. I could see it done in Federal style, with four pillars to the roof. A children's wing in place of the chicken coops and pigsties. A formal rose garden. So far, so good.

Once inside the house, I grew even more optimistic. There was an airiness, a spaciousness about the rooms; even a brightness, despite the grime on the windows. Sonny and I explored every inch of the house, ending up in the basement, where my optimism was put to the test when I narrowly missed stepping on a snake slithering across the mud floor. As I spun around, I walked right into a thick veil of cobwebs. Retreating upstairs, I decided that the first thing I'd do with the basement was scrub it and then whitewash it. After routing out the snake(s), of course.

Back outside, Sonny and I sat down on a bench under some tall maples. He asked me if I thought I could really fix the house and make it livable. I told him that I could, but it would take time. "With my imagination and your money, we'll do it," I said, making it sound more like a battle cry than a promise.

And we did. It did take time: three years and

two months to be exact, during which some part of the house was almost always in shambles. What finally emerged was a still-rambling Kentucky farmhouse with all its crazy twists and turns intact —its façade now Federal, white instead of red, and housing an eighteenth-century library straight out of a French château. So its style is, I always maintain, *pure bastard*. But we adore it. Which is why, ten years later, three of the men who helped us remodel it would be helping to build a dollhouse replica of it.

As Sonny and I sat there that first day looking up at the lovely shapes of the tall maples on our hill, he suggested that perhaps our house should be called Maple Hill. And, as I was to discover years later, another man, scarcely more than a boy at the time, had made that very same suggestion when he first saw his family's house here. The year was 1784, and it was not February, "the ugliest month," but a breathtakingly beautiful day in autumn . . .

THE ROGERS FAMILY
1 7 8 4 – 1 8 4 1

I made my way back into the past in fits and starts. An appraiser's ancient report might lead me down an unfamiliar path and then, suddenly, a recognizable landmark, and I'd find myself standing on familiar ground! A will, painstakingly handwritten, might flag my attention with its ornate beginning ("Calling to mind the certainty of death and the uncertainty of life . . ."), and its bequests ("1 axe . . . 1 stew kettle . . . 1 bay horse . . ."), and then go on to introduce me to the rest of the family: Rebecca, Nimrod, Phoebe, Sara. *Sara Littleberry!* The name practically leaped off the page. So this was the family she had married into. Little by little, I found myself back in the eighteenth century with the Rogers family. Etiquette decreed that I ride down Limestone Road toward Maple Hill in the carriage with Elizabeth Rogers, but instead I fancied myself riding alongside Joseph Rogers at the head of the caravan. For now that I'd discovered the first family of Maple Hill, I was impatient to move in and start living . . .

·

It must have been difficult that autumn day to choose the more eye-catching sight: the lush Bluegrass countryside awash with the golds and reds of the season, or the splendid caravan that was slowly but purposefully making its way down Limestone Road to the property we now call home. One had only to see the handsome, rather imperious-looking man riding at the head of the caravan, sitting so straight and secure in his saddle, to recognize him as a gentleman of quality, a member of the landed gentry. Joseph Hale Rogers was his name; he had traded his plantation in Virginia for this land in Kentucky, and now he was here, ready to begin a new frontier life. Behind him followed his most treasured possessions: his family, his slaves, and all that he had cared to bring with him from Culpeper County.

To be more specific, it included his wife, Elizabeth, and their eight children, some of whom rode with him, while the youngest sat with their mother in the elegant carriage that preceded the twelve

sturdy covered wagons carrying his forty-two slaves; old Winnie, the family cook, with her cookstove, pots, pans, and china; his overseer and his wife; a chap from Kentucky who had made this trip before with Daniel Boone and now served as Joseph's guide; a blacksmith; twelve purebred cows and a bull; twenty-four laying hens, two roosters, six sows, and two boars; an assortment of cats and dogs; seeds for the planting of corn, hemp, and vegetables; cases of his best Virginia whiskey; one wagon given over entirely to country hams, smoked and pickled doves and quail, dried and jarred fruits, meats, and vegetables; and finally, sentimentally, the chandeliers, draperies, wall brackets, and fireplace accessories from his plantation in Virginia. A place that became more precious to Elizabeth Rogers with every mile the caravan traveled away from it. They'd come slowly over mountains . . . then flashed down the treacherous waters of the Ohio River on flatboats . . . and then come back to land again, rumbling, swaying, and lurching along some uncommonly rough terrain. Although the carriage in which she rode had been outfitted to serve as a comfortable living room, there was no way it could cushion the shocks of a road that had been worn down to the limestone rock by the

hordes of buffaloes and prehistoric animals that had traveled it en route to a salt lick or watering hole.

To a woman born to one of the oldest and wealthiest Culpeper County families, this was primitive country. Why, it was only a territory; not yet a state like Virginia. Small wonder that their neighbor Colonel Preston had been so anxious to exchange his vast Kentucky land for their small but valuable plantation. He'd never even been to Kentucky himself, and furthermore, he had no desire to go. Hadn't she heard him say, more than once, "Who wants to live in a country infested with savages?"

Who, indeed? None other than her husband. But now, as she looked out the carriage window at their land, she was pleasantly surprised. The trees were magnificent. And the tall grass, at least a foot high, the breeze blowing through it, had an almost-blue cast to it. Never before had she seen grass like that.

Every detail of their journey from Virginia had been carefully planned in advance by Joseph Rogers. He had arranged for six members of the militia to guard his caravan as far as the Ohio River. And they traveled in autumn, because the water was low then; this was important because of

An Ohio River flatboat

the two weeks spent traveling down the river on flatboats. Furthermore, he had seen to it that the flatboats had not only been specially built to accommodate the extra-large wagons of the caravan but that they had covers on them as well, to keep out the rain and offer some protection from the Indians who camped along the Ohio side of the river in what was then called the Northwest Territory.

Every night en route he had seen to it that they dined as though they were still back home in Virginia. A table was set beneath a tree within a circle formed by the twelve wagons, and they were served by old Reuben and Billy, house slaves, wearing proper livery and spotless white gloves. At times like that, listening to the slaves singing around the campfire, Elizabeth could close her eyes, and with her fingers touching the familiar damask cloth and silver service, she could imagine, for a precious moment or two, that she was still in Virginia. Then she might open her eyes to see her husband passing among the slaves, giving each man a ration of his best Virginia whiskey. On such an evening she might almost forgive him for this mindless uprooting of his family. But the next day, back in her carriage and passing through country that at any moment she felt might explode with savage Indians, she would once again feel betrayed and abused.

Only Jeremiah, their oldest, seemed to appreciate how she felt. But then he'd always been more like her side of the family—a Virginian through and through. His very obvious lack of enthusiasm for frontier life widened the chasm that already existed between father and son. So nineteen-year-old Jeremiah rode only slightly ahead of his mother's carriage, while his younger brother, John, rode proudly beside his father. They were so very much alike. When the time came to dispose of the flatboats that could not be maneuvered back upstream, it was to John that Joseph Rogers entrusted their sale. And the younger boy didn't disappoint him. He proved to be a shrewd trader like his father, selling the five flatboats to a townsman in Maysville who used their timber to build a house and several barns. Now, as the caravan approached the road leading into their property, the boy was transfixed by the sight of the rich land spread out before him.

This was not the first time his father had seen it, however. Still, as Joseph Rogers looked at his land for the second time, he felt the same excitement he had felt when he first saw it that summer of 1782, when he had come here with his younger brother, Barnett, and forty of his slaves, to claim this land. He hadn't been prepared then for what he found there: a community of forty log cabins surrounded by a wooden fort. He'd looked at Barnett, and Barnett had looked at him, and then in they rode to what was called Bryant's Station. Side by side they rode, exactly as he and his son were riding now. Down the same road.

The four Bryant brothers. The thought of them made Joseph Rogers smile now. Big-shouldered North Carolinians. Simple country lads. Of course, they'd had no idea who owned the land; in typical frontier fashion they'd settled there and built a fort for protection from the Indians. He recalled the pride with which they'd let it be known that their sister, Rebecca, was the wife of none other than Daniel Boone, the most famous colonizer of them all. Nice lads.

As he heard the wagons of the caravan turning into the road behind him, he noted the great pyramids of log which were all that remained of the cabins that had once been inside the fort. The land looked so peaceful now, it was strange to remember how it had been that August evening, soon

The fort at Bryant's Station, 1782

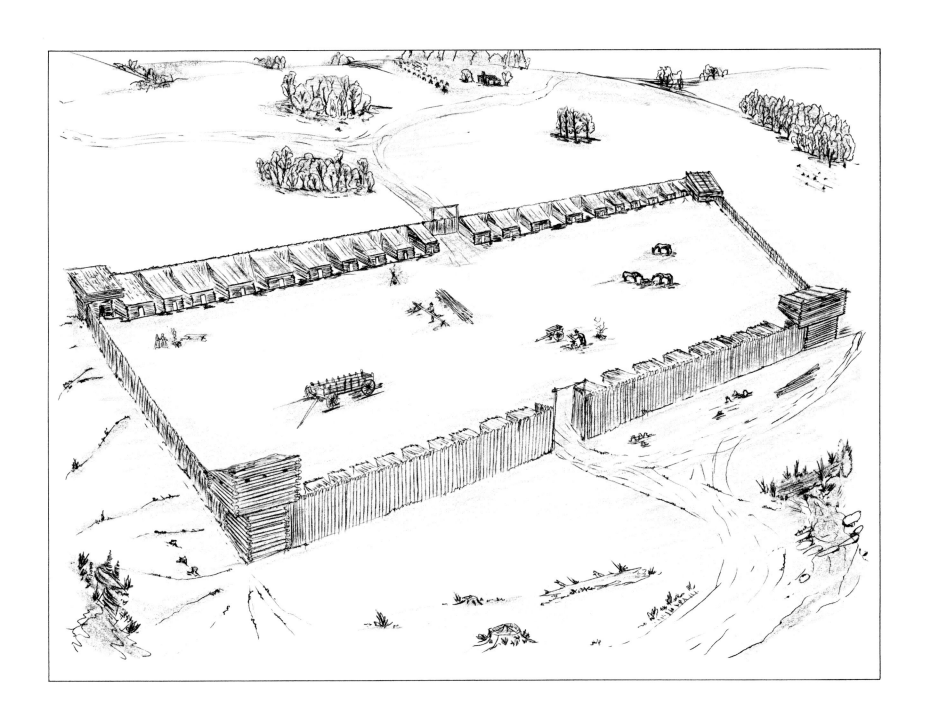

after he and Barnett had arrived, when the raiding party of Tories and Indians had attacked Bryant's Station. He wanted to remember. And he wanted to talk of it, although he knew that John had heard about it all before; many times, in fact, over the past two years. Well, he would hear it again. Now . . .

You see, boy, in the summer of '82 the war was not officially over, despite the American victory at Yorktown the year before. The Tories were still raiding settlements here in this Kentucky country, and the Indians were only too willing to help them. The Indians don't actually live in Kentucky country, but they do look upon it as their hunting ground and they don't care much for permanent settlements of white men.

Well, on that evening of August 15, about 240 Tories and Indians attacked, and for almost three days this land was under siege. Then suddenly they withdrew. You didn't have to be a master tactician to know what they were about; they wanted to lure us out into the open, where their large numbers would have the advantage. No sooner had they begun retreating than armed frontiersmen from all over this area came running into the fort. Among them were none other than Daniel Boone and his son. A fine-looking man, that Boone! He brought with him the news that a strong detachment under General Benjamin Logan was on its way; with Logan's help we'd be able to round up the raiders before they could reach the Ohio River and escape to the other side. But it didn't work out that way. The general and his men hadn't arrived by the next morning and we could see the Tories and Indians retreating into the distance, so off we went in pursuit. Well, boy, our little band stumbled into an ambush, which is the way the Tories had planned it from the start. Seventy of our men were killed or captured. Among the dead were one of the Bryant brothers . . . Boone's young son . . . and your Uncle Barnett. I buried him near the fort, but now that the fort's gone, I doubt I could find the grave. The Bryant brothers? I hear they went back to Carolina, and half the families in the fort went with them. I'm told the ones who stayed behind have all built houses around here. They'll be our neighbors. You'll be meeting them. They're good, God-fearing people. When I'd buried Barnett and made ready to return home and bring the family back here, they all came to bid me goodbye. Any minute now, boy, you're going to see your new home. And eventually each of you boys will have

a parcel of this land and you'll be building your own home on it. There's enough timber left over from the fort for that, as well as all the cabins and barns we'll need. There'll be no brick houses on this land until the last Indian is out of the area. Look over there, boy! See the corn the darkies planted before I left. It's a splendid sight now, isn't it? They'd begun to build the house, too, before I left. They were using timber from the fort. We should be seeing the house any minute now. There . . . there it is!

•

Elizabeth Rogers was leaning out of her carriage at that moment, straining for a better look at the house up ahead. Lord, couldn't they travel faster? Then the caravan halted, Jeremiah helped her down, and she had her first close look at her new home: a spacious, partly log, partly frame house. Admittedly not so grand as their home in Virginia, but agreeable enough to make her smile almost in spite of herself. Of course, she would improve it. Standing beneath the trees heavy with autumn leaves, she studied the façade, and just as I would do so many years later, she began to visualize how it would look when she was finished with it.

Young John stood beside his father, some little

John Rogers's log cabin, 1791

distance away. Looking back down the road at the fine maple trees, he said, more to himself than anyone else, "Maple Hill . . . Maple Hill." Joseph Rogers looked from his wife to his son, and then, putting his arm around the boy's shoulder, he said that that certainly sounded like a most fitting name for the house that John would soon be building on his own parcel of land.

•

Elizabeth Rogers was a thoroughbred. Somewhat spoiled, perhaps, but a thoroughbred, and so she quickly and cheerfully adapted to her new environment. She was heartened by the news that Indian attacks had been steadily decreasing, and in fact, only a few stray Indians had been sighted in recent months. She was further cheered by the part she and her husband had played in the founding of the first church in the region. It was a Baptist church, a fact of no little importance to them since they were Baptists and it had not been particularly fashionable to be one in a Virginia still largely committed to the Church of England. The Particular Baptist Church still stands, but today it's known as Bryan's Station Baptist Church. (If you visit our part of Kentucky these days, you will discover that sometimes Bryant is Bryan.)

Elizabeth was delighted, too, by the establishment of a one-room public school next to the church. Its master's practice of whipping each of the boys at regular intervals, with or without reason, was generally regarded as evidence of his good character and pedagogical fitness. "All of Kentucky," she wrote to a kinswoman in Virginia, "is full of the history of the family, not in great deeds, but in the story of its conquest from wilderness to civilization, in the work of ministry and of education."

Meanwhile, her husband was occupied educating their older sons on the cultivation of their Kentucky farmland. Its incredibly fertile soil was producing superb crops of hemp, as well as the one hundred bushels of corn per acre he had predicted when he first laid eyes on it. There was also a gristmill on the shores of the Elkhorn creek, and a fine distillery, which was considered a necessity of pioneer Kentucky living.

Predictably, John was the most energetic of all the Rogers boys. Although still only in his early teens, he went each day to the almost four hundred acres of land his father had allotted him, and with the help of the eight slaves given him, he started to clear his land, lay the foundation for a modest farmhouse, and plant crops. He had marriage on his mind. He planned to return to Virginia and marry Sarah Kirtley, a childhood playmate and cousin. His mother and her grandmother Sarah Early Kirtley were sisters. She had been only a child of ten when he had last seen her, but she was his choice, and it was in anticipation of their marriage that he built his double log cabin. Then, in 1790, six years after he'd left Virginia, nineteen-year-old John Rogers returned to Virginia to marry Sarah Kirtley. Always the dutiful son, he didn't leave Kentucky until after the harvest was in.

It was on a cold, clear day in December that John rode up to the imposing house of Jeremiah Kirtley. A fire was crackling in every fireplace in the house, and the entire family was gathered there to greet the sturdy youth, who looked so much like his father that everyone, except Sarah, remarked on it. She simply stood in the center of the living room, smiling prettily, waiting to be claimed by her husband-to-be. And just as John Rogers never disappointed his father, neither did he disappoint Sarah. Delighted with how pretty she had grown, he went directly over to her, took her in his arms, and kissed her soundly on the lips, while her family beamed approval.

On February 10, 1791, John and Sarah were married in the Baptist church in the town of Culpeper.
No known document reveals how soon after the
wedding the young couple set out for their Kentucky home. Certainly after their marriage John
was kept very busy, for, again like his father, he
carefully planned every last detail of the trip back
to Kentucky. But where his father had arranged
for six members of the militia to guard his caravan
as far as the Ohio River, John arranged for twelve,
for there had been rumors of unusual Indian ac-
tivity along the Ohio.

He and Sarah were going to be part of a caravan
almost as large and heavily laden with what Ken-
tucky-bound immigrants called "possibilities" as
his parents' had been. As the oldest daughter of
Jeremiah and Mary Robinson Kirtley, and the first
to wed, Sarah had an uncommonly fine dowry. Her
mother lavished on her beautiful linens, old silver, lovely porcelain, her grandmother's tea set, a
Britannia tea pot, twelve Windsor chairs with a
matching dining table, two Hepplewhite side
tables, an old sugar desk, four bedsteads with feather
mattresses, along with rugs, paintings, pots and
pans, bolts of wool and silk for clothes, and a goodly amount of homespun cotton. But perhaps most

precious of all was Sarah's very own crib, which
she had occupied as a baby.

Most migrations to the Kentucky frontier were
composed of several families. This one was no
exception. Captain William Kirtley, Sarah's grandfather, had recently acquired land in Kentucky,
and he and his wife, who was John's mother's sister, insisted that it be their caravan and that John
and Sarah come with them as their guests. Sarah
Kirtley would feel much safer with Joseph Rogers's
look-alike son accompanying them on what she,
like Elizabeth Rogers, considered to be a very
questionable journey. John understood her reluc-
tance to leave Virginia, for his Aunt Sarah was very
much like his mother. His stories of the happy,
prosperous life in Kentucky cheered her immeas-
urably. She was delighted to hear that her sister
had added a formal rose garden and an apple
orchard to her property, and that her sugar maples
provided a goodly amount of syrup. And Captain
Kirtley, a rugged, outdoors man, grinned at the
thought of fishing the Elkhorn creek, which, as John
told it, was literally splashing with trout, bass, and
bluegills. Kentucky certainly sounded like the land
of plenty, and by the time the caravan had started
off, both Kirtleys were looking forward to their

arrival in Bluegrass country . . . especially now that President Washington had signed the proclamation giving Kentucky statehood.

Sarah, who was now pregnant, rode with her grandmother in a fine London-made carriage, tended by a young Haitian slave girl named Tangie, who apparently adored Sarah on sight and was much loved in return. Although they traveled in comparative luxury compared to most settlers, meals weren't served with the same pomp as that insisted upon by Joseph Rogers. John would ride ahead of the caravan in search of wild turkeys and other game; then in the evening they would gather around a big open fire and eat informally with the soldiers and other members of the caravan.

It must have been a very uncomfortable trip for a pregnant woman, and often at night Sarah, unable to sleep, would crawl out of their wagon to stand outside. On such a night, a blanket wrapped about her shoulders, she turned the corner of the wagon and found herself being grabbed from behind and lifted off her feet. At the same time, a large, rough hand was clamped over her mouth. Somehow she managed to open her mouth, and when she did, she sank her teeth into the palm, drawing blood. As the hand let loose, her screams brought every man in the caravan tumbling from the wagons. Shots rang out in the night, and two bodies fell to the ground. One was a mortally wounded Indian, the other a trembling Sarah.

The next morning, as the caravan slowly made its way to the flatboats that would take them down the Ohio River, Sarah sat in the carriage, well aware that from now on her grandmother would be seeing Indians at every turn in the road. And that night, when they made camp, Daniel Boone, a friend of Captain Kirtley's, came to warn them that the float down the river would be a dangerous one. The British were once again inciting the Indians along the banks of the Ohio.

·

The first week on the river passed without incident. They had two excellent Indian guides and perhaps they were in more danger than anyone else. So they were outfitted to look like Kentucky woodsmen; Sarah and her grandmother donated face powder mixed with oil to rub on their faces in order to make their masquerade as white men the more convincing to the Indians watching from their encampments on the banks.

Then, on their twelfth day of floating on the

The kitchen

river, they saw smoke in the distance and heard the beating of drums. It was with a good deal of relief that they also saw Daniel Boone's canoe approaching. He was helped aboard, and characteristically he came straight to the point. The Indians were planning to attack their boats while they were tied up on the riverbank that evening. He said that, since it would be a full moon, they should keep on floating down the river all night.

John and Captain Kirtley sprang into action. The militia was evenly distributed throughout the five flatboats, lead was melted over the cookstove, bullets were made, powder horns filled, and the Kentucky long rifles, to which so many Kentuckians owed their lives, were cleaned and put into perfect order. Then all the men strode on deck, rifles in hand. As the boats maneuvered down the river, Sarah sat inside an unlighted wagon with her grandmother and Tangie, who sat with the conch shell she had brought from Haiti pressed against her ear. Mrs. Kirtley began to whisper the Twenty-third Psalm, and soon Sarah and Tangie joined her. "The Lord is my shepherd; I shall not want . . ."

As the three women prayed, outside, a very pretty young woman was discovered hiding in a wagon on one of the other flatboats. How long she'd been there no one knew. They knew only what she would freely admit: she was a runaway white slave. When he had had a better look at her in the moonlight, Captain Kirtley recognized her as a girl who had been bought at auction by one of his relatives and who had worked as a personal maid for the lady of the house.

A white slave was not uncommon. Many of Kentucky's earliest settlers were white slaves; redemptioners they were usually called, since they could work off their indenture. Many of them were English girls who were given free passage from England to America by boat captains, who then sold them for what their passage would have cost.

The girl refused to tell who had been feeding her since she had stowed away. Captain Kirtley entrusted her to the care of the lieutenant in charge of the twelve members of the militia. So now the lieutenant had two assignments: to keep an eye on this girl, and to keep both eyes on the lookout for Indians. Apparently this proved too much for the hapless fellow and he confessed all. The girl had run away to be with him. They planned to marry when they reached Kentucky, where no one would know she had been a slave. His confession ended abruptly when several Indian canoes were seen catching up with the fifth and last flatboat, on which the lieutenant and the girl were standing. Captain Kirtley gave the order to fire. The Indians retaliated, but the lively battle was a short one when, as the flatboats headed toward the rapids, the Indians turned their canoes around and paddled back up the river.

The next day the weary flotilla arrived safely at the dock at Limestone. There the handsome lieutenant married his slave girl, and all members of the caravan agreed that nothing was ever to be said again of the stowaway they had discovered.

At this point the caravan split up. With his overseer and slaves, Captain Kirtley traveled on to his land in northern Kentucky, where his now tearful wife was to join him once he had cleared his land and built a house. Bundling his very pregnant wife and her grandmother into the buggy he had bought before leaving Virginia, and followed by two wagons, one of which was crammed full of Sarah's fine dowry, John Rogers headed down Limestone Road toward home.

Before the little caravan was halfway to John's double log cabin, his family was running down the road to greet them. Hopping down from the buggy,

John embraced his mother and father. Then, turning around, he helped the two women down. Pick-
ing Sarah up in his arms, he proudly carried her
over the threshold of their new home where, only
a few weeks later, their first child, Ann, was born.

By 1796 there were two more children, and two
single-story brick houses were in the process of being built on a gently rising hill above one of the
more pronounced bends of the Elkhorn. It was the
very hill with the maple trees that had inspired the
name Maple Hill. The smaller of the two houses
was to become a slave house. The larger, the new
home of the growing family of John and Sarah.
And some of the logs of their former house, built
from the timbers of the old fort, began a third life
now as the ceiling beams in the cellar of their new
house. So Maple Hill, as we know it today—a main
house and a nearby slave house—became a reality.
This solid brick farmhouse of Mr. and Mrs. John
Clark Rogers and family still stands as the nucleus
of our rambling farmhouse, which is situated on the
same gently rising hill still thick with maple trees.

.

Sarah grew to love the rich Kentucky soil as much
as her mother-in-law did. And like Elizabeth Rogers, she planted an herb garden. It was there that,

one spring morning, she had her second close en-
counter with an Indian.

Her only companion at the time was a puppy
named Eagle, one of the progeny of the hunting
dogs her father-in-law, Joseph Hale Rogers, had
brought from Virginia twelve years earlier. It was
the pup's sudden low growl that told Sarah she was
no longer the only person in the garden. That
realization immobilized her, but not for long.
Turning around swiftly, she threw her trowel at
the intruder and then raced for the kitchen door,
closing it behind her and slamming a bar across it.
She quickly loaded a Kentucky long rifle, to which,
as I've said before, so many Kentuckians owed their
lives, and took up a position at a kitchen window.
She saw now that the Indian was also armed and
that Eagle was barking and jumping at him.

But let's have the story in Sarah's own words.
How happy it makes me to be able to tell you that!
It seems one day, while I was downtown hoisting
dusty olde books off the shelves at the historical
society, Jouett Redmon found a letter written by
Sarah to one of her Virginia cousins pasted on the
inside lid of a trunk belonging to his late father,
who'd been a night watchman on our farm. I
copied it word for word. So read this portion hav-

ing to do with Sarah's second skirmish with an Indian and see for yourself what a plucky frontier woman this pretty Virginia belle had become:

I was alone with that Indian for about half an hour, and all that he did was to walk around and around the house. I decided not to shoot him, unless it was absolutely necessary. I did, however, yell at him and tell him to go away and that I wasn't in the least afraid of him. This made him mad and he aimed his rifle at my darling little dog Eagle and killed him. I broke a pane of the window and took aim with my rifle, but by that time that yellow-livered Indian had taken off. We buried my darling little Eagle that afternoon and after many tears from the children and myself, John's father arrived with his litter brother. We have named him Eagle also, as they look so much alike. John and his father and all of the neighbors got a posse together, and went in search of the Indian, but he was a lone hunter looking for some meat and had evidently travelled light and fast. The men gave up after a few hours, and I have convinced them that the few marauding Indians that are left are really quite harmless. This has given John the encouragement to start

plans for the second stories of both the slave house and our house. We expect Maple Hill to really be a lovely spot in about three years. I have put mother's James River mantel in our parlor and it looks so handsome. We are adding things each day, as there are so many tradesmen travelling up and down our road, laden with brass work, shiny buckles, high-heeled slippers and brocades, even ruffled shirts, knee britches and wigs. We truly feel now that we have in Kentucky the same traditions of good living that we had in Virginia.

A lovely letter, I think, and a revealing one. Many of the settlers of the Bluegrass were from Virginia, and most of them tried their best to build houses like those they had known in the Old Dominion and to create a similar way of life. Some historians see this as a certain snobbishness. Perhaps so; but surely there are worse traits. Pride would seem to be a very necessary ingredient for people struggling to make a good and graceful life for themselves in an often alien environment. And just think how much progress had been made since the days of the fort at Bryant's Station. It was

The table, set for dinner

people like these who were responsible for that progress.

I just know that Elizabeth Rogers must have felt very proud when she looked from the windows of her home and saw the improvements John and Sarah were making on their property. By 1800, both Maple Hill and the slave house had acquired second stories. Imagine how excited these two gentlewomen would have been had they been able to see into the future to the day when an English princess would be a houseguest in, of all things, the slave house!

By 1804, there was another child and three more rooms, giving Maple Hill the internal pattern it would retain for the next thirty-five years or so. These additions provided the second floor with a master bedroom, and the main floor with another parlor for Sarah and a small office, with its own outside door, for John. Today John's office is the bar, Sarah's second parlor is the book room (we often speak of it as the green book room), the original kitchen is Grandmother's Room, the room my mother occupied until her death in 1973, and the original parlor is the butler's pantry in the real house and the kitchen in the dollhouse. As for the

Sarah and John Rogers's brick house, 1800

original three small bedrooms, they are now my bathroom, my husband's bathroom, and my husband's back hall with its numerous closets. To be perfectly frank, I have sort of mislaid the master bedroom added in 1804, but it's still around somewhere.

Like the James River mantel mentioned in Sarah's letter, many of the chairs, beds, and tables at Maple Hill in 1804 had come West from Virginia with John and Sarah. Other furnishings they purchased from the peddlers traveling Limestone Road. As a rule, no money changed hands during these transactions. On one occasion John traded a few bottles of the best whiskey his distillery could produce for a large wrought-iron bell. The Rogerses hung the bell outside the kitchen door. They used it to call the slaves in from the fields, and sometimes Sarah rang it on Friday nights to summon John and the boys, who usually spent those evenings at the home of John's brother Joseph across the pike.

It would seem that these original occupants of Maple Hill had a happy and useful life. John prospered as a grower of tobacco and hemp and as the owner of a fine dairy and cattle herd. From time to time he drove into Lexington to do jury duty. In those days the court was often held in the parlor of John Keiser's Indian Queen Tavern, and can't you see John ensconced in one of that hostelry's high-backed hickory chairs, a solidly built man with what, as the years rolled on, was no doubt an increasingly patriarchal manner and appearance.

He had begun his life as a farmer with the eight slaves given him by his father. His will listed twenty-one, and other records show that for several years the number was close to forty. These figures suggest that on occasion he went to Lexington to attend the auctions at Cheapside, Kentucky's largest slave market and the one that not too many years later would attract the troubled attention of a tall, raw-boned Illinois lawyer named Abraham Lincoln, a native Kentuckian, who, following his marriage to Lexington-born Mary Todd in 1842, was a frequent visitor to the Bluegrass region.

Sarah spent much of her time outdoors. She created, near the front of the house, a formal rose garden around a sundial. She helped with the installation of an elaborate grape arbor and added trees to the apple orchard that her mother-in-law had begun.

So far as I can tell, Sarah and John had the pleasure of seeing all of their children, five girls and five boys, grow to adulthood. When Jeremiah, their oldest son, married Margaret Stapleton, they deeded sixty-six of their acres along the Elkhorn to him, which reduced their own property to about 320 acres.

Ann, their firstborn, married John B. Buford and moved to his plantation in Woodford County. Daughter Elizabeth's marriage to Garland Smith placed her only a mile or so away from Maple Hill on a farm along what is now called the Paris Pike. Two of the other daughters were married in a single year, Emily to John H. Moore and Clarissa to a distant cousin, William Early Rucker. What a year that must have been! Coming as I do from a family of daughters, I think I know. And old histories tell us that in the early nineteenth century Kentucky weddings were lively affairs.

As a rule the ceremony took place just before a late-afternoon dinner. This was a feast: beef, pork, fowl, whole shoats, lamb, venison, every sort of vegetable, and sometimes "Kentucky burgoo," a delectable native stew still frequently consumed at large gatherings in Kentucky and especially at the uproarious political rallies for which the commonwealth is famous. After dinner the guests danced three- and four-handed reels or square sets and

jigs. These capers usually continued all night, save for an interlude at about 9 or 10 p.m., when the young ladies "stole" the bride and put her to bed, after which a deputation of young men corralled the groom and "placed him snugly beside her."

An old church history points to a crisis in the lives of John and Sarah. An entry in the records of the Particular Baptist Church, which his parents had helped to establish, reveals that on March 11, 1811, the Rogerses and several of their slaves were excommunicated. Possibly pertinent to this development are some passages in Richard N. Collins's *History of Kentucky* (1874). Collins writes that about 1800 some members of that church and other Baptist churches in Kentucky began exhibiting "Unitarian beliefs." During the next several years a number of members and in parts of the state entire churches withdrew from the General Union of Baptists, a Kentucky-wide association, because of their ministers' refusal to espouse the cause of abolition on the grounds that it was "improper" for men of the cloth "to meddle with the emancipation of slavery or any other political subject." Those who left as the result of this schism called themselves "Friends of Humanity."

Is it possible that John and Sarah Rogers were a part of this revolt? Who can say? All the record shows is that they were "excd." for circulating a letter "calculated to make a new party in the church" and to create "discord among black members."

For Maple Hill, and indeed for all of Kentucky, 1833 was an eventful year. It was the year of the cholera, the first of the two great plagues to sweep the state during the nineteenth century. It was also the year that saw the marriage of the Rogerses' youngest daughter, Sarah, and her removal to Lexington, Missouri, where her husband, Charles Scott Tarleton, became a successful and a renowned judge.

And it was the year of Sarah Kirtley Rogers's death. It was this unhappy event that gave rise to the still often-told story of the Haitian slave Tangie.

Tangie, you'll remember, made the long journey to Kentucky with John and Sarah. During the intervening years she had nursed and helped rear the children. One of her tasks, as they became old enough, was to take them to the fields, for John wanted his children to learn the "intricacies of farming" at an early age.

Tangie's wedding gift to John and Sarah had been the conch shell which was the only thing she had brought to America from her native Haiti. She cherished it because, when she held it to her ear, she fancied she could hear in it the roar of the sea as she had heard it during her childhood on that Caribbean island.

Tangie also claimed to know voodoo. She told the Rogerses that she had placed a magic spell on the conch shell. As long as they kept it, she said, they would know good fortune.

It tells us a good deal about John and Sarah that they took Tangie's statement seriously. All during their life together, the conch shell rested on their bedside table.

It was still there when Sarah died on May 5, 1833. But at the funeral the following day, Tangie was not among the mourners. According to legend, when she learned of her mistress's death, she walked down to the banks of the Elkhorn, drew a knife from the front of her dress, stabbed herself, and fell into the water.

John gave orders that no effort be made to recover her body. He remembered Tangie asking Sarah where the waters of the Elkhorn went and being told that eventually they flowed into the

Atlantic Ocean. Tangie, John told himself, had gone home to Haiti.

•

He found Maple Hill a lonely place without Sarah. His big farm needed a mistress to see to it that the house slaves performed the countless daily chores such a place required. Milk must be separated, cottage cheese made, butter churned, eggs candled, chickens plucked, hams cured, vegetables and fruits canned. To say nothing of Edward, youngest of the children, who at age twelve still needed someone to remind him to comb his hair and wear his boots when it rained.

John called on the Reverend Thomas Dudley, the white-haired pastor of his church. Does this visit mean that John had made his peace with the church? Perhaps. I can't say for certain. In any event, the Reverend Mr. Dudley understood the problem. In those days it was the custom for a farmer who lost his wife to replace her as rapidly as possible.

Mr. Dudley had a suggestion. It so happened that a Mrs. Dorothy Carson, a widow from Missouri, was visiting relatives in the Bluegrass region. She had been coming to church with them and Mr. Dudley had made inquiries about her.

"A fine reputation," he assured John, "and an absolute genius with the needle." Most important of all, according to the minister, the lady's late husband had owned one of the best dairy farms in Missouri. There was simply nothing about that sort of work his widow didn't know.

An introduction was arranged. John was not exactly smitten with what he saw. One glance at this plump and daintily dimpled lady told him that she would never be the strong pioneer wife his Sarah had become. But then, he reasoned, Bluegrass Kentucky was no longer the backwoods. Civilization had overtaken it, and great swales of bluegrass, that wonderful plant that seems to have been imported from England, had long since replaced the wilderness. Physically the lady before him couldn't hold a candle to Sarah. But at sixty-one, he reminded himself, a man does not go looking for the love of his life.

And so John Rogers and Dorothy Carson married before Sarah had been gone a year. The second Mrs. Rogers was an excellent housekeeper, and although the gardens bored her, she made certain that the slaves took care of those Sarah had started.

Still, for almost a year the marriage had its ups and downs. John was largely at fault. Consistently, rigidly, he refused to let his new wife make any changes in the house. And certainly that must have made her feel like an interloper. So who can blame her for deciding one morning to bring matters to a head?

This she accomplished very deftly. She simply took Tangie's conch shell from the bedside table and hid it. When John demanded to know where she had put it, she refused to tell him.

That morning they had their first full-scale quarrel. It also turned out to be the storm that clears the air. It ended, I know you will be pleased to learn, with John carrying his amply proportioned wife upstairs and depositing her on their four-poster bed. Then he shut the bedroom door behind them, simultaneously shutting out from his life forever the intruding memories of his beloved Sarah. It marked the beginning of a splendid second marriage.

I can only add to this engaging tale that, in their newfound happiness, the elderly couple forgot all about the conch shell. It wouldn't be seen again until six years after John's death, when Walter Rode, while helping to take an inventory of the estate, found it standing on one of the kitchen shelves.

•

On July 15, 1839, the *Kentucky Gazette,* the oldest of the Lexington newspapers, carried the following obituary notice:

> Died in this county on 22nd of June, Mr. John
> Rogers, in the 67th year of his age. Mr. Rogers
> was one of the oldest residents of the state, having
> emigrated with his father, while the country was
> a wilderness; he always maintained an enviable
> character for honesty and integrity and has left a
> numerous circle of relatives and friends, to treas-
> ure up his precepts and profit by his example.

His father, Joseph Hale Rogers, had died at the
age of ninety-four, only five years before. Joseph's
wife, Elizabeth, had died many years earlier, and
Joseph had remarried twice and had sired a son by
each of his wives, his last son born when he was
already seventy-four years old. His relations with
his oldest son, Jeremiah, had not improved with
the years. They were apparently as far apart at the
time of his death as they had been that day they
first arrived in the Bluegrass country. Jeremiah,
then sixty-nine years of age, was omitted from his
father's will.

*Pickled mahogany breakfront and
Momoyama screen on the sun porch*

Although he and his father were very much alike, John had a far more generous spirit. His will showed that. Over the years he had presented fifteen of his slaves as wedding presents to his children. In addition, he had provided each of the boys with some land and with a sum of money. His will stipulated that the remainder of his estate was to remain intact until his youngest son, Edward, reached the age of twenty-one. At that time it was to be disposed of by means of a dispersal sale. Exempt from this provision were the remaining slaves. The will stipulated that they were to be divided among the members of the family and that none was to be sold.

The receipts from the dispersal sale, when it took place in 1841, totaled $47,000. At that time sheep were selling for a dollar a head, turkeys for $37\frac{1}{2}$ cents apiece. According to my rough figuring, the estate of John Rogers would be worth $1,750,000 or more in today's soft currency.

Among the items sold was Tangie's conch shell. It brought the rather prestigious sum of $1.37½. After all, its new owner could have got a sheep and a turkey for that. I can't tell you who bought the shell. As luck would have it, the purchaser's name is the only one on the list to be illegible; it seems to read "Pal." Today one of our family jokes is that the buyer of Tangie's shell may have been more of a pal to the Whitney family than he intended to be. Only a few years ago one of our children came across a beautiful conch shell in the basement of Maple Hill. Tangie's? We like to think so. For several years the children argued over just which of them owned it, and at the moment it stands on the shelf of the pine hutch cabinet in our Kentucky kitchen. And, of course, the miniature pine hutch cabinet in Cornelia's dollhouse has a miniature conch shell on top of it.

As for Maple Hill, on September 2, 1841, it became the property of Willis and Harriette Thomas Muir.

THE MUIRS
1 8 4 1 – 1 9 2 6

The people of Bluegrass pronounce the name Muir as though it were spelled "Mwire," frequently dropping the M, so that it comes closer to sounding like "Wire." And although that has the effect of clipping what should be a soft, leisurely sound, it comes closer to expressing the personality of the Muirs of Maple Hill, a lively, colorful people who lived there for eighty-five years. The Muirs of Maple Hill guided me back into the twentieth century, and much as I enjoyed wandering through the Kentucky of the distant past, I was happy to be back. For several reasons. The record books were far less dusty. Pages were typewritten and easy to read. But, most of all, because now I was visiting with fascinating people who were kind enough to share their memories with me. I was particularly fond of one courtly gentleman who had known

Willie T., the last Muir to live at Maple Hill. He brought him vividly back to life for me: Willie T., a blithe spirit if ever there was one, racing the country roads in his cream-colored touring car. "Oh, but I was years younger than Willie, you understand," this gentleman informed me, giving his starched cuffs a snappy tug.

Willis Muir, the son of a Scottish immigrant who had arrived in this country in time to serve in the Revolutionary War, and his second wife, Harriette, took up residence at Maple Hill in the autumn of 1841, along with their six daughters, three sons, one son-in-law, and a retinue of slaves. The Muirs were high-spirited, hard-working, and fun-loving.

Willis loved horses. And one of his earliest additions to the grounds was a perky cast-iron jockey painted with the Muirs' racing colors. It's still there. For pleasure he bred and raced trotting horses. For profit he concentrated on saddle and livery stock for sale to people living north of the Ohio River. He also started a herd of shorthorn cattle that, as subsequently developed by his sons, was reckoned one of the finest in the area.

Harriette loved parties, and she gave plenty of

them. Summer was the ideal social season in the
Bluegrass. During the warm months, planters from
the Deep South crowded into the Lexington area
to enjoy its milder climate. On many a summer
night the parlors of Maple Hill, stripped of their
rugs and arbored with flowered trellises, echoed to
the stomp of couples dancing to the fiddles of a
hired orchestra, laughing, chatting, and quenching
their thirst with mint juleps served in cups crafted
by Willis's kinsman George Muir, a well-known
Kentucky silversmith. Afternoon lawn parties fea-
tured a popular local concoction composed of lem-
onade and bourbon in about equal proportions.

During the 1840's, the Abraham Lincolns of Illinois were frequently in Lexington, staying at the
Main Street home of Mrs. Lincoln's banker-politi-
cian father, Robert S. Todd. As one of the Muirs'
close friends, Mrs. Margaret Preston, had roomed
with Mary Todd at boarding school, it's very likely
that on occasion the future First Lady and her
husband participated in the festivities at Maple
Hill.

For the socially minded Muirs, the house as they
found it was much too small. Within a year they
had expanded it considerably, bringing the façade
closer to Bryan Station Road and giving the house

The terrace. The wrought-iron furniture is
all handmade. On the table under the poplar
tree is a handmade set of sterling-silver
julep cups

the front line it would have when I first laid eyes on it more than a century later.

It was the Muirs who installed the stairway that now sweeps airily up the southern wall of the entranceway. They added a third parlor, one of the glories of which was its elaborate woodwork, hand-carved by the slaves. The new parlor had a spacious bay window overlooking the Elkhorn, and from this window one had a view of a circular drive rimmed with pale-blue iris and climaxed, as it were, by a large carriage step, a rectangular stone from the rock quarry, with the cast-iron jockey standing beside it.

On the other side of the entranceway the Muirs put in what is still the formal dining room. I have Harriette to thank for moving Sarah Rogers's James River mantel from one of the old parlors to this bright and cheerful place. The second floor got two new bedrooms, one of which is now my husband's bedroom and the other the sitting room, where, during our stays in Kentucky, I spend most of my mornings working at an old French desk gilded with ormolu.

As these improvements neared completion, the Muirs suddenly had a reason to want them done even sooner than planned. Shortly before they had

moved into Maple Hill, Elizabeth, Willis's eigh-
teen-year-old daughter by a previous marriage, had
become the wife of Lawson G. Webster, a young
farmer whose parents had been among the log
cabin settlers of Bryant's Station. By early 1842 she
was pregnant, and Willis and Harriette urged her
to have the baby at Maple Hill. Now the question
was, Would at least one of the new rooms be ready
before the arrival of Willis's first grandchild? It
was, and Laura Webster was born in April in a
bedroom on the second floor. But on the twenty-
eighth of that month, Elizabeth died. And if a
curious local custom was followed, on the twenty-
ninth or thirtieth, one of the house slaves, prob-
ably old Tab, hitched up the family barouche and
delivered at the doors of the Muirs' friends black-
bordered "funeral tickets" reading: "Yourself and
family are invited to attend the funeral of our
daughter . . ."

Elizabeth Muir Webster may have sensed that
death was coming. I've been told that not long before the birth of her daughter she expressed the
wish that, when her life was ended, she be buried
near the rose garden at Maple Hill. Her grave is
still there. During the 1950's, when Maple Hill had
become a near ruin, Elizabeth's grave seemed to be

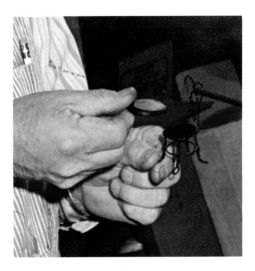

the only thing in that part of the farm that was being properly cared for. I assure you that it still is.

As for little Laura, no child was ever more deeply loved. I understand that the Muirs' second-oldest son, Thomas, who never married, devoted a good portion of the rest of his life to a not wholly unsuccessful effort to spoil her.

Like John Rogers, Willis Muir was a wealthy man when he died on June 12, 1850. To his wife he left one hundred acres of his land, "including my mansion and other improvements, and all household and kitchen furniture, and the following slaves, Randall, Tab, Amanda, and the grey mare Polly." Under the terms of his will the remaining acres were divided among the three boys, and they and Harriette were to supervise the estate. In addition, $2,000 went to each of the surviving daughters and $1,000 to granddaughter Laura.

The records are exceedingly blurry concerning the ages of Harriette's sons at the time of her husband's death. Most genealogies list William first, followed by Thomas and Samuel, and other evidence indicates that their ages ran from nineteen to twenty-three. All three of them helped with the management of Harriette's portion of the property, with the bulk of these duties falling on William and Thomas in 1852, when Samuel married a girl named Ann from Jessamine County and moved into a modest house on his share of the land near the Dripping Springs section of the Elkhorn.

At the time of Willis Muir's death, the Civil War was a decade into the future. Yet any astute individual living in Kentucky during the 1850's must have worried greatly about the divisiveness that the slavery question was causing within this border state. Here the defenders of slavery and its opponents met head-on. Fathers and sons fell out. Brother opposed brother, neighbor, neighbor. A brother, three half-brothers, and the husbands of three half-sisters of Mary Todd Lincoln joined the Confederate forces, while a brother and a half-sister remained loyal to the Union.

In early 1861, much to the relief of Kentucky-born Lincoln, the state proclaimed itself officially neutral. But in actuality it quickly became one of the more active battlegrounds. During the course of the conflict, sixty-four thousand of its sons served in the armies of the Union and thirty thousand in those of the Confederacy.

Even those parts of the Bluegrass remote from the roads used by the troops were vulnerable to straying bands of soldiers belonging to both sides and to roaming gangs of rascals bent on taking advantage of the confusion to rob and pillage the countryside.

At Maple Hill Harriette saw to it that hams, flour, jarred fruits and vegetables were stored in the tunnel that still connected the main house to the slave quarters. Her instructions to the house blacks, Randall, Tab, and Amanda, were to take refuge there should trouble start. With their assistance, she wrapped up her smaller valuables and hid them in crevices or buried them near the smokehouse on the southern lawn.

One balmy spring morning the inevitable occurred. The story, as I have it, is that granddaughter Laura, now a pretty girl of nineteen, and her father were visiting neighbors and that the Muir brothers, William and Tom, were planting hemp at a far end of the farm when Harriette, at work in her vegetable garden, spotted a couple of Yankee soldiers coming toward her.

They were faster than she. Before she could run to the house, the two men had twisted her arms behind her back and were pushing her toward the kitchen door.

Fortunately, Amanda had seen what was happening through a kitchen window and had rushed down to the tunnel, where Tab and Randall were stacking provisions. Randall took off at once. Getting to the slave quarters by way of the tunnel, he let himself out through the back door there and then raced across the fields to where William and Tom were working.

Meantime, in the house the two soldiers used their weapons to prod Harriette from room to room, cursing repeatedly as it dawned on them that little of value was around. Harriette noticed that Amanda was not in the kitchen and the thought occurred to her that help might be on the way, so the longer she could keep the soldiers in the house the better. When they demanded to know where she had "hidden things," she pointed upstairs.

The intruders pushed Harriette into a closet in William's room upstairs and bolted the latch on the room side of the door. Plainly they weren't well-trained soldiers, for had they looked around, they would have seen that William kept some of his hunting rifles in the closet.

Harriette waited until the silence on the other side of the locked door told her that the men had moved on. Some matches she found in a pocket of one of her son's jackets gave her enough light to

The living room

load a gun. A knife and a hairpin enabled her to lift the bolt and step out.

In the hall she listened for the sound of the men's voices. One of them had obviously gone back downstairs. She could hear the other one pulling out the drawers of the big chest in her bedroom. Clutching the gun, she tiptoed to the open bedroom door. The man inside had put his gun on the top of the chest. Suddenly seeing her there at the door, he reached for it. Harriette fired, killing him instantly.

At almost the same moment a shot rang out below. As she would learn later, the other soldier had heard William and Tom coming in at the back and had fired in the direction of the kitchen. Other blasts followed, and hurrying downstairs, Harriette found the second soldier dead on the Brussels carpet of her dining room.

Thus ended the Battle of Maple Hill. It's not known just how the bodies of its victims were disposed of. Harriette Muir announced that "under no circumstances are those two Yankees to be interred on my land." According to the present minister of Bryan Station Baptist Church, the Reverend Mr. Alfred M. Gormley, they now rest somewhere behind the church building.

The war ran its course, to be followed by the troubled days of Reconstruction. Tradition has it that, when in 1865 the ratification of the thirteenth amendment put an end to slavery, Randall, Tab, and Amanda remained at Maple Hill. They went on doing the same old jobs, living as they always had in what after the war was referred to as the servants' house rather than the slaves' quarters.

Harriette was in her sixtieth year when death came on August 27, 1871. By this date several changes had overtaken the Muir family. Samuel was no longer living on the Maple Hill lands. He and his family moved down the Bryan Station Road to a large farm that they had purchased from James B. (Gentleman Jim) McCreary, twice governor of Kentucky. Bachelor Tom had moved into a house of his own at the Paris Pike end of the farm. Originally erected by one of John Rogers's brothers, Tom's new home had been so vastly enlarged by previous tenants that people spoke of it as the Waldorf Astoria. I don't know where granddaughter Laura and her father were residing at this point, but it's possible they were at the Waldorf Astoria with Tom.

William Muir would pass the whole of his adult life at Maple Hill. At the time of his mother's

death, he had been married for some time, and in
the fall of that year the occupants of the house once
again experienced the poignancy of birth followed
by death. On September 12, William's wife, the
former Mary V. Turner, died while giving birth to
a daughter, who received the name Lula and who
lived for only four months.

William and Tom continued to work and pros-
per together. By 1871 they were the owners of
twelve hundred acres in their home county of Fayette, and of another twelve hundred acres in ad-
joining Scott County. Their practice was to divide
their time between the two places, and it was in
Scott County that widower William made the ac-
quaintance of Mrs. Mary E. Thomas Kenney, a
winsome widow and the mother of a little girl
named Emma. Friendship soon ripened into love,
and before long William was carrying his second
Mary across the threshold of Maple Hill.

Let me confess here and now that the more in-
formation I gathered about Mary E. Muir, the
fonder I became of her. What sort of a woman was
she? Well, she was certainly not a good business-
woman. She was forever leasing portions of the
farm to people who took advantage of her. She was
sometimes exasperating, often stubborn, and always

romantic. Perhaps it was the romanticism that got to me. Friends tell me I lean in that direction myself.

It was Mary E. who decided that the time had come for Maple Hill to be given a "face-lift." The times were Victorian. And up and down Bryan Station Pike and Paris Pike great gobs of gingerbread and Everests of irrelevant towers and turrets were beginning to brighten the landscape, or to blight it, depending on your taste. Away went the Georgian look that the Willis Muirs had given Maple Hill. A large porch materialized across the front. I gather that it was a marvel of fretwork and bric-a-brac. High above it a saucy gable topped Maple Hill's first, and so far last, third floor.

I'm told that Mary E. got the idea for this addition when some Scott County friends, invited to have a look at her fashionable new porch, informed her that without what they spoke of as a "third-floor gabled room" no house could be "truly chic."

In the beginning William was less than enthusiastic. "A third floor consisting of only one room?" he is reported to have grumbled. "What a waste of time and lumber!"

Mary E. hastened to point out that she planned to use the room for sewing. She spent much of each

day sewing, and what a joy it would be, she said, to sew in a room high enough so that from time to time she could look out the window and watch her husband at work in the fields.

Of course, Mary E. got her gabled room. Indeed, her adored and adoring husband gave her more than she had hoped for. He saw to it that the room was finished with hand-hewn cherrywood logs, held together by wooden pegs so as not to mar their glowing surface.

The changes in the house were not limited to Victorian froufrou. I think I detect William's practical hand in the decision to install a new system for directing rainwater from the roofs into a cistern dug at the back of the house and capped with a large pump.

In 1876 Mary E. presented her husband with a daughter, Lida T. The child lived for only three years, but by 1880 two healthy girls, Sallie and Mary A., and a sturdy little boy had been born. As a toddler the boy had a fine head of red hair and a twinkle in his eye, both of which would remain with him throughout life. Their name for him, William Thomas, was quickly shortened to Willie T.

Mary E. loved her husband dearly. Too dearly,

Maple Hill in 1880

it would seem. For when he died in 1890 she refused to recognize that he was gone. She would sit for hours in the gabled room, sewing or standing at the back window, certain that any minute now her husband would come walking in from the fields. Over and over, her bachelor brother-in-law, Thomas, would take her to the cemetery in Lexington, show her the grave, and tell her in his patient, kindly way that she would never again see William in this world. She only half believed him.

Poor long-suffering Thomas. In 1898 he finally decided that the time had come to put more distance between himself and his difficult sister-in-law. He sold her his share in the Maple Hill lands for $910, closed up the Waldorf Astoria, gave up farming on a large scale, and retired to a small place at nearby Muir Station, where he died at age seventy-eight, leaving a will that distributed his ample estate among his brothers and sisters and their heirs.

At Maple Hill Mary E. was never alone, however. Residing with her since the close of the Civil War was an uncle, Alexander Thomas, a gentlemanly old man who tried hard to exert a steadying influence on Willie T., who at an early age gave signs of becoming something of a hellion. All of

Mary E.'s daughters had married, but for many years after William's death, Emma, the oldest, and her husband, D. M. Herndon, lived at Maple Hill.

The Muirs' love of a good time still prevailed. There were dances in the parlors and parties in the apple orchard. Mary E.'s interest in these affairs, however, was marginal to the point of being non-existent. She continued to spend most of her time in the gabled room, sewing or standing at the back window.

Neighbor women were persuaded to keep her company, and I'm indebted to two of them, Mrs. Charles Fredericks and Mrs. Julian Frank, for telling me about those long, strange days in that paneled room with the dark-green window shades that were drawn to the windowsill when the sun became too intense. From them comes the picture of how, to the end, Mary E. refused to abandon the conviction that her husband would return, and of how with the passing years her always slight body took on a kind of elfin frailty.

Almost her only tie with reality was her son. She worshipped Willie T. She refused to be annoyed by his passion for driving his cream-colored touring car up and down the pikes at what for those days, and on those roads, was breakneck speed.

And she dismissed with spirit the constant and apparently accurate stories of his frequent and often costly appearances at the gambling tables of Lexington.

On March 5, 1910, apparently without his mother's knowledge, Willie T. took himself a wife. His bride, Edna Gianni, was a resident of Lexington and the daughter of Arthur Gianni, a well-known architect from Cincinnati, Ohio. I get the impression that Edna, a personable and easygoing young woman, was exceedingly well liked in the neighborhood by everyone . . . except her mother-in-law.

There was an emotional explosion when the news reached the ailing prisoner of the gabled room. Mary E. told her companion at that time, Mrs. Fredericks, that "I cannot abide Edna. She'll never be the mistress of this house!" The old lady added that she was going to change her will. Previously she had intended leaving the whole of her estate to Willie T. Now she planned to leave everything to charity.

As a matter of fact, when Mary E. joined her beloved William in February 1916, the first will to be presented to the authorities was not quite that drastic. The surviving records and newspaper ac-

The desk in Mr. Whitney's bedroom

counts of this document are inconsistent, but I gather that under its terms Willie T. was to enjoy half the estate for the rest of his life. On his death, all of it was to go to the University of Kentucky for the education of students preparing for careers in the Christian Church.

But in death, as in life, Mary E. bungled. Willie T. and Edna went to court and there they produced another and more properly attested-to will that left everything to them.

In 1917, Willie T. and Edna moved into Maple Hill. One of their first acts was to board up the staircase to the third floor. After that, I understand, it was a matter of principle with them to act as if the gabled room had never existed.

At first Willie T. raised thoroughbred horses, producing some good racers and winning a few ribbons in shows. Then he turned to livestock, and finally to general farming, but none of these activities really interested him. He was happiest away from home, working for the Democratic Party or for the Christian Church, or racing his car up and down the pikes. No children appeared, and after almost ten years of trying with little success to make a go of the farm, he and Edna sold it in 1926 and moved into Lexington. There, until his death in 1961, Willie T. helped manage the old Kentucky Hotel, a job that suited his convivial nature.

Willis and Harriette Muir would have adored their grandson had they known him. Everybody liked Willie T.

THE MARSHALLS,
McDOWELLS, AND
SANDUSKYS
1926–1951

I approached my research of this period at Maple Hill with a fair amount of trepidation, especially when I discovered that it had changed hands *three* times in nineteen years. So I prepared myself for the worst. After all, I had the benefit of hindsight and, unlike the Marshalls, who had bought Maple Hill in '26, I knew the Great Depression was just around the corner. So many lovely homes went to seed then. Of course, I hadn't reckoned with Bliss McDowell, whose husband bought Maple Hill in '31. She wasn't one who would permit anything so temporarily devastating as an economic depression to undo the charms of her home. Hadn't she one night, long after she and her husband had sold Maple Hill, come back and . . . Oh no, I mustn't tell you about that now. Not when you're going to read all about it just a few pages on . . .

By the time John D. Marshall and family bought
Maple Hill, the land had been reduced to two hundred acres. But the soil was still incredibly rich
and the Marshalls, who already occupied a dwell-
ing on the Paris Pike, happily farmed it for the
next five years, although they actually lived in it
for only a relatively short period of time.

Climbing a ladder one day, one of the Marshall
boys peered into the gabled room on the third floor
and was properly impressed with the cherrywood
paneling William Muir had put there when he
added the room which his wife wanted so very
much. The room was now inaccessible since Willie
T. had boarded up the staircase, but this didn't
faze this enterprising young fellow. The room
didn't interest him, but the cherrywood certainly
did. So he proceeded to remove it, piece by piece,
and carried it through the small front window off
the third floor and down the ladder. It eventually
made a handsome table and other items of furniture.

In 1931 Maple Hill was sold to Joe Desha Mc-
Dowell and his wife, Bliss. She proved to be a very
spirited lady with the same sort of intense love of

home and hearth that Sarah Rogers, Harriette Muir, and (why be shy?) I all shared. So the very first thing Bliss McDowell did was to remove the gabled room on the third floor that had seen so much unhappiness during its short life span and restore the peaked roof to its original line. Happily, the passion for things Victorian had paled, and Mary E.'s large porch, that marvel of fretwork and bric-a-brac, was replaced with a plainer, far more suitable one.

Maple Hill was 140 years old now and still didn't have any modern conveniences. Fireplaces and stoves heated the rooms. There was no inside plumbing, and one still bathed in a tin tub kept in one of the first-floor closets. *"Scandalous!"* I can imagine Bliss saying, as she set about to remedy the situation. A Lexington firm, Fitzgerald Plumbers, put in a furnace and a central heating system, and then went on to install three bathrooms, one of which went into the small back hall room that had been used by Mary E. for her staircase to the third-floor room.

Bliss adored trees and flowers. Willie T. and Edna had neglected those on the property, and the Marshalls, so occupied with farming the land, had simply ignored them. Bliss brought them back to

life: She had all the diseased trees removed by Louis Hillenmeyer, the surviving ones pruned and sprayed, and then she added a variety of new ones. Soon a splendid grape arbor stood exactly where Sarah Rogers's had once stood. Bliss replenished the herb and vegetable gardens, and planted perennials in the old rose beds. Now, with the bluegrass always smartly clipped and all the vegetation flourishing again, Maple Hill was once more a showplace.

There's a charming bit of mystery attached to one of the changes that took place during the McDowells' occupancy. The exact year I don't know, but sometime during their days at Maple Hill they permitted United States government engineers to place a plaque near the outside door of the dining room at a point on the line crossing the country where the compass point on north is accurate with no deviations, which is to say, on a point where true north and magnetic north coincide. Still in the same spot today, the plaque carries a legend reading, "There is true north and magnetic north. There is no deviation from the compass of Truth."

Bliss McDowell surrounded the plaque with a circle of bricks, and obviously the memory of it lingered on long after she and her husband sold

One of the upstairs bathrooms

Maple Hill in 1945. By the time my husband became the proprietor of the house, Joe Desha Mc-
Dowell had died, but his wife, who lived to be
eighty, was still in the neighborhood.

During our renovation of the house, it became
necessary one evening to remove the plaque and
place it overnight in the safe in the farm office. At
about eleven o'clock that evening, the night watchman, as he rounded the front of the house, saw a
figure in flowing black dropping down from the
wall alongside Bryan Station Road. As he watched,
puzzled, the "apparition" (his word) crouched mo-
mentarily among the rose bushes around Elizabeth
Muir Webster's grave and then wafted to the din-
ing-room door.

When he turned on his flashlight, he saw, kneel-
ing there, a very old lady with a spade in her hand.
The beam of his flashlight brought out the pierc-
ing quality of her eyes as she called to him, de-
manding to know where "the compass plaque" had
gone. When he told her it was in the safe, she
moved swiftly away, fading into the darkness.

The next morning one of the women working in
the farm office took a telephone call. A cracked
voice informed her in no uncertain terms that
unless the plaque went back to where it belonged

*The Queen Anne coffee table on the sun
porch*

the owner of the voice would see to it that it was placed on display in a local museum.

We never checked on this strange occurrence, but I assume that Bliss McDowell was satisfied with our handling of the compass plaque. To this day, it rests in its original spot, a low circle of bricks around it.

The McDowells sold Maple Hill to the Sandusky family in 1945. They had spent fourteen very happy years there, and I'm fairly certain they would have remained indefinitely but for the fact that they were getting along in years and it was simply much too big for them to handle.

The Sanduskys lived at Maple Hill for six years and during their time did not do any renovating to the house and grounds. I understand that they raised some livestock and that they did some farming. I'm told they added a very beautiful wrought-iron gate at the front drive, but it went with them when they sold Maple Hill to my husband in 1951.

With the purchase of Maple Hill and its two hundred acres, the C. V. Whitney farm next door became a perfect square of exactly one thousand acres of some of the most beautiful and fertile land in Bluegrass country. It was this great pastureland that Sonny wanted, for he needed more room to rotate his cattle, his corn, and his tobacco crops. The house he wanted to renovate and use as his home whenever he was in Kentucky. But he wasn't to move into Maple Hill himself for another seven years, and meantime he would rent it to friends of his.

THE KIRKPATRICKS,
BENNETTS, AND
WHITNEYS

1951–1975

❧

Sonny loved Maple Hill, but it simply wasn't possible for him to live there at the time he bought it.
So for the first seven years he owned it, this lovely
old house had a variety of tenants. So many, in fact,
that I couldn't find records for them all, and few
stayed long enough to make the house feel loved.
I think that even inanimate objects "feel" love and
in their own way respond. Although it had sur-
vived the Depression years in fine shape, due to
the loving care of Bliss McDowell, by the mid-
1950's Maple Hill was vacant and in the most dis-
reputable shape. As you already know, Sonny more
or less dared me to make it livable again, and I
accepted the challenge. I became something of a
fanatic, fiercely protective, when it came to Maple
Hill. I fought to protect every last bit of it. The
first time I saw detergent bubbles floating down

the Elkhorn, I hopped into my car and sped to the county courthouse to file a complaint. I kept coming back, too, so often that they began referring to me as Marylou Pollution. Another time I stalked out, gun in hand, and threatened road crews about to chop away at our maple trees. For I knew something of what our house had been through in recent years, and I was determined to love it back to health.

·

Haden Kirkpatrick, owner of *The Thoroughbred Record,* a weekly publication often spoken of as the "horse bible," and his wife, Ann, were Sonny's first tenants. The house at that time was almost completely covered with thick vines. It looked beautiful, but it was wholly impractical, for the old bricks had become.so porous that in some corners of the house small mushroom-like growths began appearing. Still, the vines were put to practical use on at least one occasion by, of all things, an enormous snake.

Standing in the apple orchard one day, Haden looked up and saw the reptile slither from a vine into a window air conditioner on the second floor. Haden had a quick response: he ran into the house and upstairs, where he promptly turned the air conditioner on full blast. Then he telephoned an electrician and reported that the machine was acting strangely.

When the unsuspecting electrician arrived, he turned off the air conditioner and began to remove its cover, as Haden watched warily from the hall outside, fully expecting to see a snake, or pieces of a snake, emerge. It was admittedly a little late in the day to tell the man the real reason he had been called, but as he gave the cover a final yank, Haden yelled out to him to beware of the snake. But although there was no sign of a snake, the blades of the fan were completely bent. I have no idea what Mr. Muse's response was to Haden's last-minute warning, but I do know the snake was never found. Later, when I started renovating the house, we discovered dozens of snake skins in the attic. Apparently this poor snake was simply trying to get up there to shed his skin and the air conditioner expedited the job.

Tom Bennett and his wife, Helen, were Sonny's next tenants. They lived there for several years, during which time the house really bloomed again. The Bennetts entertained a great deal, and I don't imagine Maple Hill had been so gay since the days when Harriette Muir gave her fabulous parties. So it was fitting, I think, that the Bennetts should have discovered the cast-iron jockey the Muirs had brought with them to Maple Hill in 1841 and painted with their racing colors. Somewhere along the way the little jockey had been misplaced and forgotten. The Bennetts went to work on him with rust remover, and then painted him in their own racing colors. They stood him back on his pedestal and placed him by the old carriage step, where he had stood so many years ago.

Tom and Helen Bennett loved Maple Hill and wanted to buy it from Sonny, but he refused, still hoping to live there himself one day. The Bennetts eventually bought a beautiful house across Paris Pike and moved out. After that, various tenant farmers lived at Maple Hill, and later some factory workers from IBM rented it. Then it was vacant and remained vacant, for it was no longer in any condition to be lived in. Still, that didn't stop Sonny from wanting to live there. And perhaps if the house hadn't looked as desperate as it did, I wouldn't have been so passionate about restoring it.

I became extremely possessive about Maple Hill and had no intention of working with an architect. Furthermore, I suspected that no self-respecting

architect would permit me to preserve some of the idiosyncrasies of our funny old house. Three rooms, for example, without any outside windows. And I wasn't about to let anyone hack out those fine old walls to insert a window.

Sonny and I decided that Maple Hill certainly needed a new façade. In its long life it had gone through a Georgian period, a Greek Revival, and even became a Victorian "monster" by the end of the nineteenth century. Our brother-in-law George Headley drew the designs for a Federal façade and we adored it on sight. It was wildly unconventional, however, since the one-story columns on either side of the front entrance were not connected with the two-story middle columns. And while an architect might have gone along with our "floating" columns, I imagine that he would have insisted that we do *something* with the back and middle part of the house, which are of the Georgian period John and Sarah Rogers loved so dearly. We did do *something* with it; we kept it intact.

We added some things, and got rid of others. I closed off the slave tunnel leading to the slave house, for instance, and dug out part of it to make the laundry room bigger. We added a children's wing, consisting of four bedrooms and two baths,

on the second floor. (We haven't added this wing to the dollhouse yet, but expect to do so very soon.) Another Whitney addition to the house is the oak-paneled library that I told you about earlier. It came from a château in the south of France; Sonny and I spotted it at the Scearce Wakefield Galleries in Shelbyville and simply had to have it. Maple Hill is such a happy mix of so many periods, I could see nothing wrong with adding an eighteenth-century French room to an early-American farmhouse.

Somewhat to the northwest of the house, where those chicken coops and pigsties had been, we also added a new building, a large glass-topped structure that resembles a Roman atrium and houses an Olympic-size swimming pool. It was here we held our reception for Princess Margaret and Lord Snowdon. We built a bridge over the swimming pool, and floated on the water several illuminated swans fashioned of white carnations and ostrich plumes.

Brother-in-law George obligingly took to his drawing board once more and came up with a modern version of a smokehouse, which we built on the very spot where the original had stood overlooking the mill pond. You'll recall that it was near the limestone underpinnings of the smokehouse that Harriette Muir had hidden the family silver during the Civil War. Sonny and I have turned our smokehouse into a studio, and we often go there and spend an entire day painting. Sonny speaks of his paintings as "dramatic realism." I just paint . . . mostly children and animals.

By the time we had moved into Maple Hill, Sarah Rogers's grape arbor had become so ragged and overgrown that I replaced it with a rose garden. I don't think Sarah would have complained. Her apple orchard is still a magnificent sight. I thought of her in 1969 when we played host to the thirty-three governors who had come to Lexington to attend the Republican National Governors' Conference. The governor of her beloved Virginia was among them.

I think that it's fair to say that we worship the Elkhorn creek. Sonny stocked it with rainbow trout and our Louella fries them with hushpuppies for us, just as Tangie used to do for Sarah and John. About a half mile from the house the Elkhorn divides around a tiny island. Here Sonny had the workmen put up a picnic table with benches under a small shelter. Many a morning, even a snowy winter morning, driving along the nearby

road, I've seen him sitting there by himself, staring contentedly into the swiftly passing water.

Once the main house was the way we wanted it, I turned my attention to the slave house, which is now a charming, self-contained guest house. Since Princess Margaret and Lord Snowdon stayed there, we've been calling it the Princess Margaret House. And no sooner had we completed Cornelia's dollhouse than we began to construct a tiny replica of the Princess Margaret House. As I write this, it's just been completed and it's perfectly enchanting.

It has two floors, a brick terrace to one side, and trees and shrubs made of sugarcane painted green that are the most realistic I've ever seen. Particularly charming is the tiny replica of the upstairs bedroom Princess Margaret used. It's so feminine with its blue silk chaise longue piled with lace and brocade pillows, pale-blue bedspread embroidered with pink flowers, and the box of American beauty roses and asparagus ferns open on the bed. This dollhouse even has a tiny storage room downstairs full of bric-a-brac and furniture: old lamps and lamp shades, a teddy bear, a flat iron, a fish aquarium, pitchers, a Shaker basket full of wood, a telephone book, and even a broken white marble bust of Jefferson.

The upstairs bedroom in the guest house. The draperies and bedspreads are of Fredericksburg design; the beds, bedside tables, and dressing table of eighteenth-century French design. A box of American Beauty roses is open on the bed, as if to welcome Princess Margaret, who used this room during her visit to Kentucky.

Yet in building this dollhouse we goofed. The iron bars on the original are outside the windows; on the dollhouse they're inside. But none of us really minds. Who knows, someday this little goof may give to the Princess Margaret House the added value that a typographical error has sometimes been known to give to a new postage stamp.

As every woman knows, a home is never altogether finished. And neither is a dollhouse. I assume we'll never stop making changes and additions to keep it an exact replica of the real house. And there's repair work to be done, and mini-scaled housework.

Window drapes, for example, tumble down and have to be pasted back. Dust gathers on the tiny tables and must be whisked away with a tiny duster. Silver must be polished. And Cornelia and I have become rather expert at upholstering the tiny furniture.

To work inside the dollhouse one must lift the electrical hoist that permits the outside walls to be raised, unhinge the internal partitions, and crawl into the space between the upstairs floor and the roof. You really have to be something of a contortionist to work in that cramped interior, and if I've gained a pound I know it.

Looking into the downstairs bedroom of the guest house

Cornelia and I have discovered still another pleasure in having a dollhouse. When the urge comes to rearrange furniture in the real house, or replace some shrubs, we experiment first with the tiny replica. If we like the new look there, then we go ahead and make the change in the real house.

I don't believe anyone ever outgrows the enchantment of a dollhouse. I know I never will. Whenever I'm away from Kentucky and return home, I unpack and then head straight for the Shed Row Foreman's cottage where Cornelia's dollhouse stands. I raise the hoist, turn on all the lights in the tiny house, and then walk slowly around it. I never really feel that I'm home until I've done this. I can't give the roof of the real house a loving pat, but I can the roof of the dollhouse. And I do. Often I imagine I see Sarah Rogers standing by her beloved James River mantel, or Harriette Muir fussing about in a bedroom on the second floor, getting ready for a party. Certainly if a dollhouse can house a ghost, it must be Mary E., floating about, searching for the missing third floor with its gabled roof.

Maple Hill has known sadness, but basically it's a very happy house. A much loved house. Somehow I think the dollhouse expresses this on sight, in a way that only something so tiny and compact can. Something so tiny can be, I think, profound. A poem of only a few lines often says more than pages of text. And I look upon Cornelia's dollhouse as a kind of love poem dedicated to Maple Hill and the people who have lived there.

I hope that one day both our dollhouses will stand in a museum where children can enjoy them. For its children have been such a happy part of Maple Hill, from the Rogers children, who arrived by covered wagon, to our brood of five, who, no longer children now, sometimes arrive by jet. They always come back here for Christmas no matter how far away they happen to be. Maple Hill is home. And the dollhouse with its tiny Christmas tree and holly wreath on the front door is home, too, in miniature.

Small enough to be taken in at a glance and committed to memory.

Small enough to be tucked away in a corner of your heart.

CORNELIA VANDERBILT WHITNEY'S DOLLHOUSE

The parquet floors are made of walnut. These were made from old window frames from Maple Hill. This wood was first used to build the fort at Bryant's Station in 1779. The second time it was used to build John Rogers's log house in 1789. The third use was for the building of Maple Hill in 1796. Its fourth use was for the building of the dollhouse in 1968.

There are 630 pieces of wood in the floor. The three rugs are a Kazak pattern and are handmade. There is a five-branch crystal and brass chandelier. The newel post is made of cherry and oak from the old fort.

The Hepplewhite table (1785–1800) is set with a pair of sixteen-tapered candelabras (originals at Palace of Versailles) and a gold clock under a dome. The mirror is a Philadelphia mirror (1820–30). There is also a mahogany three-gilt-finial grandfather clock and an American shield Hepplewhite chair.

The Empire-style draperies are in gray satin with gold tassels and cords and have crimson satin valances.

The Aubusson rug is a petit-point copy of our original one, which is Louis Philippe, and it lies on a parquet floor that contains 2,790 pieces of old walnut.

The chandelier has over 1,200 tiny crystals and is eighteenth century in design. The crystal three-branch wall sconces complement it.

The marble mantel is a Victorian one, with an Adam Eagle and Swag mirror (1785–90) over it. The andirons are Louis XVI brass ones and the fender is a James River one. On the mantel is a gold Victorian clock, flanked on both sides by a lady and a gentleman under glass domes. To the left of the fireplace is a pole fire screen with a mahogany pedestal and hand-painted roses on black lacquer.

The Queen Anne tea table with candle slides (1735–50) has a pair of Duncan Phyfe chairs on either side. It is set with an eighteenth-century China-trade tea set on an old English tea tray.

On the Chippendale table, next to the Sheraton green-striped sofa, is a silver Statue of Liberty, a *Gone with the Wind* ruby hand-blown glass lamp, an Oriental black-lacquered box, and a gold filigree ashtray.

The eighteenth-century Hepplewhite swell-front commode has hanging above it a Hepplewhite filigree mirror, a pair of pale-green Venetian vases on top, and a white marble "Bust of a Boy" in the middle.

The French Empire circular sofa in pink satin has a center column of gray marble and is topped with an antique urn holding a very French bouquet. There is a hand-painted gray tomcat on the sofa.

The Empire sofa in the Phyfe style has on its left a pie-crust Chippendale table with a large orange-and-white-flowered Persian vase filled with dogwood, also a fine Japanese silk fan and a pair of gold lorgnettes. On the opposite side is an eighteenth-century three-tiered table with carved snake feet. On it you will see an Imari blue and white bowl, a blue hand-blown glass pitcher, a Victorian flowered paperweight, and a hand-carved Chinese coral dog. On the coffee table is a large silver Sheffield tray with two filigree ashtrays and a white apple compote filled with lilies and Shasta daisies. On either side of the table is a fine pair of Queen Anne winged fireside chairs (1745–60).

The square piano is about 1840, with a stool of the same period. It can be wound to play music. On top of it is a fine Eagle China-trade punch bowl and a pair of seventeenth-century tall ruby Bohemian lusters. The two side chairs are Duncan Phyfe.

The gilt harp has seven pedals and is actually positioned on E flat. The eighteenth-century music stand next to it has brass candlesticks with movable arms.

There are six oil paintings copied from original early-American primitives. They are titled "Portrait of a Woman with White Fischu and Cap," "A Basket of Fruit," "Child at Prayer" (early 1800's), "Child with Doll," "Man with White Ascot," and "Lady in Blue." There is also a pair of lovely kakemono Oriental scroll prints.

This dining room was added to the house by Harriette and Willis Muir in 1850. The fireplace mantel is the James River one Sarah Rogers had in her parlor in 1801. The parquet floor contains 1,620 pieces. The rug is a miniature copy of a Kazak.

The table is Hepplewhite (1785–1800) and is set for eight with a George III epergne (original by William Cripps, 1757) and a pair of English candelabras circa 1762 and two Queen Anne candlesticks, Old English silver water goblets and wineglasses. The silver service plates and Colonial flat silver were all handmade. The crystal compotes have silver bases. The napkin rings and dinner bell are Victorian, and the salt and pepper shakers are Georgian. There are twelve Duncan Phyfe side chairs, and a Chippendale pie-crust tilt-top table.

On the Hepplewhite sideboard are a Victorian silver cake stand, a George III well-and-tree platter (original by William Hunter, London, 1764) with matching carving set, a sauce boat (original by James Richardson at Metropolitan Museum of Art) and a pair of Crown and Swag bonbon dishes.

On the mantel are a pair of Old English three-branch candelabras and an oval, covered, silver, footed bowl. Over the mantel is a Philadelphia 1820 mirror. The andirons are eighteenth-century brass and the gilt fireback is shaped like a fan.

On the Sheraton card table there is a champagne bottle with tiny ice cubes in a silver bucket, and a Chippendale serving tray, circa 1770, with a teapot, a sugar bowl, and a creamer by Adrian Bunker (original

Yale Art Gallery). The sugar tongs are 1800. On two matching Sheraton tables are a pair of Georgian, covered vegetable dishes with gadroon edges (originals by Paul Storr) and a pair of Old English three-branched candelabras.

The draperies of blue silk taffeta are in a Fredericksburg design, with tiny tassels and tiebacks. The brass wall sconces are eighteenth century, and the five-branch chandelier is a James River one.

The oil paintings are hand-painted on very fine linen; the originals are in the Boston Museum. One is an American primitive titled "A Fine Gentleman," another is "Boy with Horse" (1830). There is also an antique daguerreotype framed in a crisscross gold frame. The pair of gilt mirrors are Georgian, circa 1760.

The oval braided rugs are all handmade. There is a Cape Cod wing chair and a pine hutch cabinet. On top is a miniature basket of wild mustard. There are cookbooks and a China-trade eighteenth-century bowl.

There is an old pine Sheraton drop-leaf table on which is a pewter plate and a country ham on an old platter. Nearby is an old pine washtub, scrub board, coffee grinder, etc. Every cupboard, the refrigerator, and the stove are full of cooking utensils, canned goods, preserved fruits and jams, meats, cereals, and herbs, etc. Over nine hundred items!

There are green gingham curtains at the windows, and pots, pans, and a calendar hanging on the wall.

On the yellow-tiled floor is a great-grandmother hand-woven rag rug.

The breakfast table, of Italian wrought iron, is set with 1840 Dresden china. There are service plates, egg cups with eggs, hot-chocolate cups and saucers, and early-American flat silver. The chairs in black wrought iron are also Italian.

On the pine side table is a Dresden platter and soup tureen filled with wild white roses. The inlaid side table has a Victorian hand-painted glass plate with French bread and a glass dome cover.

The oil paintings are a pair titled "Basket of Flowers" and "Basket of Fruit."

The china cupboard is filled from top to bottom with Dresden china.

In front of the two Hepplewhite sofas is a Queen Anne coffee table. On it is a fine Bohemian ruby glass decanter set (about the seventeenth century) sitting on a Chippendale tray. There are also a hand-painted Venetian glass plate, a fluted silver candy dish, and a variety of magazines.

On the eighteenth-century drum table in the corner are a George III silver picture frame (original by Robert Adam, London, 1767), a live fern that lives on air in a brass urn, a covered glass candy jar full of candy, and a goldfish aquarium. On the other drum table are a picture in a Victorian brass frame, a Venetian glass plate, and calla lilies in a green and pink cache pot.

The 1760 breakfront is in pickled mahogany. On its shelves are an eighteenth-century China-trade teapot, a sugar bowl and creamer, and two pink Chinese bowls. Also, there are bridge pads, pencils, a crossword puzzle book, and Webster's dictionary. Behind the breakfront is a magnificent Momoyama Oriental screen (circa 1575). The subject of birds and flowers is inherited from Chinese masters. The brilliant colors, however, are reminiscent of the earlier Yamato-e scrolls and manuscripts. One part of the design, the waterfall, is quite Chinese, whereas the pattern as a whole, which contrasts the pine and its needles in the background with the rocks and water in the foreground, could only be Japanese. The rocks, quite apart from the role they play in the composition here, have many Chinese predecessors, but the light wash in gold patterns is uniquely Japanese and affords an astonishing amount of depth. All these elements combine to create the unusual effect of gorgeous color and composed dramatic line that typifies a Momoyama screen painting.

The chairs around the pickled Sheraton card table are Hitchcock (1840). On the table are a game of checkers and a Chinese lacquered box containing two full sets of playing cards.

The inlaid table next to a sofa has a green telephone and a directory. The other small table is a Sheraton stand, and on it is a very old and beautifully carved ivory abacus.

The oil painting is a seascape called "Cape Cod Harbor Scene with Lighthouse."

The old porch is redone in wormy chestnut and has a wagonwheel chandelier. On the floor is a handmade, round, braided rug.

The oval gateleg table (circa 1700) is in mahogany and is set with blue Onion ware service plates, pewter flatware, and three China-trade eighteenth-century ginger jars in the willow pattern. The chairs around the table are pine ladder-back with rush seats.

There are two captain's chairs on either side of a drum table, which holds a green glass-shaded reading lamp.

The old pine, hand-rubbed Welsh dresser contains a collection of pewter spoons, plates, bowls, and a large teapot. On the top are two pots of African daisies.

On the walls are a pair of early New England sconces of old pine with brass reflectors and bayberry candles. There is also a sampler, "Home Sweet Home." The hanging pine gun rack holds one single and one double-barreled shotgun with fine walnut stocks; they have the same balancing as real guns. In the corner is a pine coat rack holding a man's cane.

There are two Louis XV Aubusson rugs. They were popular in this country during the Colonial period and, again, during the Empire period. The parquet floor contains 1,640 pieces.

The red and white toile draperies are of Fredericksburg design, and this print is used in other places in this room.

There are two Staffordshire dogs on the fireplace hearth in front of an eighteenth-century Regency fire fender. The two eighteenth-century candlestands are holding a pair of 1812 brass candlesticks. On the mantel are a sterling-silver race horse and two silver trophy cups with gold-washed insides. A silver brook trout mounted on a plaque is above on the wall.

The two early–Queen Anne wing chairs are covered with tan leather, and opposite them are a mid-eighteenth-century Chippendale sofa, two cherry and leather corner chairs (1725–75), and a Chippendale coffee table, which has on it a round silver tray (original by Paul Revere, 1761) with a sherry decanter, two silver goblets, and a variety of magazines.

On the pie-crust table are a green Victorian reading lamp, a silver porringer (circa 1700–20), a silver sugar pot (original by Thomas Savage is at Yale University), and a Sheffield silver pot filled with white tulips.

The three-tiered table with snake feet has on it a Sheffield silver pitcher, a dried-flower arrangement in a gold filigree pot, a Delft pitcher, and gold opera glasses.

Next to one of the fireside chairs is an 1810 sewing stand with pipe, lighter, ashtray, and picture in Victorian frame.

On the Empire table are a bronze bust of Josephine, a China-trade blue and white porcelain bowl with an Oriental dried arrangement, and a very old hand-carved Chinese Buddha, a gift of George Headley. On the floor is a hand-painted world globe on a standard.

The seventeenth-century library table has, in front of it, a Queen Anne chair. On the table are busts in white marble of a boy and a girl, a book on Nathaniel Hawthorne, a brass inkstand, and a letter blotter. Above it hangs an Empire half-spindle mirror.

There is a very fine reproduction of George Washington by Gilbert Stuart over the sofa. The other oils are titled "Lady with Green Sleeves," "Man with a Monocle," "Five Mast Sailing Boat," and "A Winter Scene." There are also two Revival shadow portraits.

There is a very fine collection of miniature books that are all readable. Among them on the bookshelves are hand-painted wooden duck decoys, a uhlan helmet, and a Dragon helmet.

The following is an index to the books:

Wood's Illustrated Almanack for 1844. London. 1½ x 1. Orig. pictorial wrappers, much darkened. 11 engraved plates. Complete.

Petit Paroissien De L'Enfance, Le. L. Lefort, Lille. n.d. 1½ x 1. Orig. pink wrappers. Rubbed. Small hole in back cover.

Small Rain upon the Tender Herb. Am. Sunday School Union. Phila. (c. 1855). Full red morocco, wallet flap. 1⅜ x 1⅛.

Bryce. *The Smallest English Dictionary in the World.* Glasgow. n.d. In the original metal case.

Crowther (Alice; editor). *Golden Thoughts from Great Authors.* Glasgow, David Bryce, ca. 1900. Maroon leather binding, 128 pp. 26 x 19 mm., 1 x ¾. Quotations from Shakespeare, Coleridge, Phillip Sidney, Dr. Johnson, Dryden, and others.

Koran in Arabic. Orig. cloth, worn. 1¹/₁₆ x ¾. The type carried by the Yemeni as a charm against evil.

Gasc (F. E. A.). *The Smallest French and English Dictionary in the World;* Glasgow, David Bryce and Son; London, George Bell and Sons, ca. 1895, original red roan, in original metal case with inset magnifying glass, 648 pp. on fine india paper, 29 x 20 mm., 1⅛ x ¹³/₁₆ inch, now very scarce.

English Bijou Almanack. Schloss. London, 1836. ¾ x ½. Orig. white and gold binding with green onlays. Fine.

Janka (Gyula). *Miniatur konyvek tortenete es gyujtese.* (The history and collecting of miniature books.) With illustrations; Budapest, Egyatemi Nyomda kollektivaia (collection of the University Press), 1969, most attractively bound in white richly gilt-stamped plastic, front cover in three red and blue panels, 81 pp. 21 x 17 mm., ⅞ x ¹¹/₁₆.

Marx-Engel. *A Kommuniste Part kialtvanya.* Kossuth Konyvkiado. 1971. 1⅜ x 1⅛. Full morocco. Fine.

Kis Kepek Nagy Muvekrol. Budapest, 1967. 13 color plates of famous paintings. 1½ x 1¼. Full morocco.

Small Pictures of Famous Paintings. Budapest, 1967. 1⅝ x 1⅜. 13 color plates. Full morocco.

Petit Paroissien, Le. Firmin Didot, Paris. n.d. 1⅛ x ⅞. A cheaply produced little book printed rather crookedly, so the binder has shaved some tops. Embossed brass cover with green silk back.

Arion 3, Poetry for Everybody. Edited by Somlyo Gyorgy. Excerpts from the *International Almanack of Poetry* published by Corvina. English and Hungarian texts; Budapest, 1970, attractively bound in black cloth with light-blue panels and gilt fillets, 109 pp. 30 x 22 mm., 1³/₁₆ x ⅞.

Lincoln (Abraham). *Addresses.* Kingsport, Tenn., Training Division, Kingsport Press, 1929. Original red Niger morocco, gilt edges, (8), 139 pp., colophon leaf. 22 x 16 mm., ⅞ x ⅝.

Petit Paroissien de la Jeunesse, Le. Marcilly, Paris (ca. 1825). Gold stamped white glazed bds. Orig. slip case (mended).

Leopardi (Giacomo). *Dialoghi.* One of 250 copies printed; Florence, Libreria del Teatro, printed by Artigianelli, 1943, original leather, raised bands, 78 pp. 22 x 16 mm., ⅞ x ¹¹/₁₆.

Dewdrops. London, n.d. 15th ed. 1⅞ x 1¼. Black leather with wallet flap. Crosspiece missing, otherwise fine.

Small Rain upon the Tender Herb. London, n.d. Second ed. 1¼ x 1¹/₁₆. Full red morocco, gold fillets.

London Almanack, The. 1810. 1³/₁₆ x 1⅛. Full red morocco, loose in binding. Lacks lower half of clasp.

Nodier (Charles). *La filleule du Seigneur.* Histoire du chien de Brisquet. Contes. Illustrations par M. Moisand; Paris, Pairault, 1897, stiff lilac wrappers, 66 pp., 5 pp. advertising other volumes in this "Collection Miniscule," 39 x 30 mm., 1½ x 1³/₁₆. Fine unopened copy.

Hitler (Adolf). *Der Fuhrer in den Bergen.* Bilddokumente von Heinrich Hoffmann. 24 photo plates by Hitler's official photographer. No place, Winter-Hilfswerk des Deutschen Volkes (1936), original stiff wrappers, photo of Hitler in his mountain retreat on front cover, 8 pp. of text. 50 x 35 mm. 1¹⁵/₁₆ x 1⅜.

Lenin. *A Magyar Tanacskogtarsagrol.* Kossuth Konyvkiado. 1968. 2½ x 1¾. Full red morocco in board case.

Small Rain upon the Tender Herb. London, n.d., 7th ed. 1¼ x 1. Inscription dated 1834. Red morocco, wallet flap.

Meydenbach, J. *Strange Fish.* 1970. 1³⁄₁₆. 64 p. format.

Levien, J. *Noah's Ark.* 1970. 1³⁄₁₆. 64 p. format.

Levien, J. *Arche Noah.* 1970. 1³⁄₁₆. 64 p. format. In German.

Levien, J. *Business Worries.* 1970. ⅞. 16 p. format.

Levien, J. *Enjoy Life.* 1970. ⅞. 16 p. format.

Levien, J. *Tribute to Sig.* 1970. ⅞. 16 p. format.

Levien, J. *Have a Cigarette.* 1970. 1³⁄₁₆. 24 p. format.

Levien, J. *A Child's Bible.* 1970. 146 p. format. 1⅜.

Levien, J. A set of five titles all 1³⁄₁₆, all 16 p. formats; titles are *Smart Cat, Book of Doom, Get Well, Enkhuizen,* and *Tower of Babel* (in 11 languages).

Levien, J. *Family Quotations.* 1970. 1³⁄₁₆. 24 p. format.

Levien, J. *Nativity Story.* English, 1971. 10⁄₁₆ x 7⁄₁₆. 32 p. format.

Levien, J. *Geboorte Verhaal.* Dutch, 1971. 10⁄₁₆ x 7⁄₁₆. 32 p. format.

Levien, J. *Christi Geburt.* German, 1971. 10⁄₁₆ x 7⁄₁₆. 32 p. format.

The book room can be seen through the library door. Its green-and-white-floral hand-hooked rug lies on a parquet floor made of 1,300 pieces of wood.

The fireplace is Victorian marble with a nineteenth-century black-wire fire screen, brass-ball andirons, and black iron tools.

The Queen Anne sofa is done in green chintz and has three wing chairs to match. On the side table are a green lamp, a telephone, a directory, and a green Venetian bowl. A hand-blown ruby glass decanter sits on the inlaid coffee table alongside a hand-painted candy jar. On the walnut drum table is a bust of Thomas Jefferson in white marble.

The Queen Anne desk has a leather desk set, a reading lamp, and a Queen Anne desk chair.

In the back hall beyond are a Victorian fainting couch in velvet and a gold Victorian mirror.

The rug is a floral hand-hooked one. The lyre table has two blue and white willow-design ginger jars and a blue and white China-trade footed bowl on it. The mirror is Empire. The chairs are Duncan Phyfe. On the Victorian commode is a Sheffield silver coffee pot full of dogwood, flanked by two fluted silver bowls. The mirror is Federal with a brass eagle.

The two original oil landscapes were painted in St. Augustine, Florida, by Mrs. Holmes of the Copper Cricket Gallery, and the miniature harp is Victorian.

Covering most of the floor are a log-cabin-pattern hooked rug and a great-grandmother hand-woven throw rug.

The Sheraton 1790 bed has a point d'esprit lace spread. The 1810 bedside table has a telephone, a directory, and a Dresden pitcher.

The Sheraton dressing table has a dresser set of pink bisque, an early-American mirror with a hand-painted scene, and two early brass candlesticks. The Hepplewhite swell-front eighteenth-century dresser has a 1750 dressing mirror on a stand. There are also a family album, a Venetian basket of flowers, and a pair of seventeenth-century, low, English, brass candle-sticks. Next to the Lincoln rocker is a double-door pine sewing stand.

An early banjo clock hangs on the wall; also two Godey fashion prints, 1873.

The draperies are in rose silk taffeta with deep curved cornices and tiny silk tassels. The floor is covered with wall-to-wall pale-pink shag carpet. The chandelier is James River, with an elaborate cut crystal and gilt center.

There is a Victorian white-marble mantel with an American gold inkstand clock on it. Also, there are two gold Victorian fans. In front of these is a pair of tall Bohemian ruby lusters with clear prism drops and tapers (nineteenth century). The andirons are brass eighteenth-century ones, and the high serpentine fire fender is Regency.

The chaise longue is of rose silk taffeta with assorted lace and velvet pillows. Next to it is an 1800 candlestand with a rose-pink telephone. The matching stand on the opposite side of the fireplace has an 1812 candlestick.

The hand-painted dressing table with mirror has two hand-painted Venetian perfume bottles with matching tray, a sterling-silver hand mirror, a gold-leaf silver jewel box, and a tiny enameled ring box with a hinged top opened to reveal a diamond ring. The Queen Anne dressing-table stool is in striped satin. The gray mother cat on the floor is carrying a kitten in her mouth.

The half-round mahogany table has beautiful ormolu, and the mirror is an Empire half-spindle one. On the table are a large Dresden pitcher and basin full of lilacs.

Between the two velvet silver chairs is an inlaid coffee table with a Victorian-period exotic bird under a glass dome, a live fern in a brass pot, a silver night candleholder, two Dresden ashtrays, and a flowered writing pad.

The French desk with ormolu has on it a desk set, including a plumed pen in a striped glass inkwell, a brass pot full of tulips, a silver compact, and a brass nineteenth-century candlestick. The desk chair is striped satin with a Hepplewhite shield back, and the Queen Anne stool is in matching fabric.

The oil painting over the mantel is titled "Child with Doll" (early 1800's), and there are two miniature oval paintings of flowers. A painting entitled "Basket of Flowers" is over the dressing table. The two Godey fashion prints are 1862 and 1865, and the other two prints are eighteenth-century flower ones.

There are Fredericksburg rose silk taffeta draperies at the windows. The floors are carpeted in pale-pink nylon shag. The chandelier, although simple, is handsome with its four branches.

The 1790 American four-poster bed has tester rails in cherry. Its canopy and spread are made of eighteenth-century antique-finish satin of flame stitch in rose and green. The corner bedside table has a tall Limoges vase filled with lilacs. The other bedside table has a pink telephone, a Louis XVI candlestick, and an old wedding photo in a Victorian brass frame. At the foot of the bed is a Hepplewhite window seat (1785–1800) upholstered in striped satin.

The metal fireplace is a nineteenth-century coal one with a coal grate and silver fire tools. On the mantel is a silver urn with a turquoise top, made in Taxco, Mexico. On either side of it are two silver racing trophies filled with tulips, and a pair of very fine old floral China-trade bowls (eighteenth century). By the fireside is a rose-colored chaise longue.

The fruitwood commode has ormolu trim; above it is a Victorian gold mirror. On the commode are a pair of candlesticks, a large eighteenth-century French clock, and a gold perfume set of Federal design.

Between the windows is a prie-dieu made of cherry and upholstered in antique-red velvet, with a velvet cushion and a tiny Bible.

Above the fireplace is a tinsel painting, circa 1837–50. It is made of tin foil behind glass which is crumpled to catch the light and add a silver glow. On either side are two tiny miniatures, hand-painted, of a boy and a girl. Also, there are a late eighteenth-century flower print and two very fine silk Japanese fans.

Above the Chippendale highboy is an Empire mirror. Hanging near it is a very beautifully made barometer with hygrometer (original by John Beale, Southampton, England, eighteenth century). On top of the highboy are a pair of old English brass candlesticks, a glass apothecary jar filled with stick candy, and Mr. Whitney's camera.

Hanging on the walls are two fine maps—one of Nantucket and the other of Bermuda—also a pair of eighteenth-century bird prints.

In the far back hall are a Sheraton table with a Duncan Phyfe side chair, a Venetian glass vase filled with lilacs, and a very old print titled "Cardinals."

The floor has wall-to-wall carpeting in a floral design. The windows have mustard-colored silk Federal-style draperies.

The mantel is Victorian, and has brass-ball andirons, a Regency fire screen, brass and wrought-iron fire tools, and a brass wood basket. On the mantel are busts of a boy and a girl flanking a late nineteenth-century clock. Over the mantel is a Federal mirror with a brass eagle.

The maple four-poster bed is pegged and roped instead of having springs. It is circa 1830 and has a white hand-loomed spread with a blue dust ruffle. The eighteenth-century blanket chest at the foot of the bed is covered with assorted magazines and photo albums. The bedside table is an eighteenth-century drum table with an alarm clock, a yellow telephone and a directory, and a silver ashtray with fluted edge.

There is an Empire commode with a 1750–75 dressing glass on a stand, a silver night candlestick, a silver thermometer, and a silver cologne bottle. The two armchairs and ottoman are in yellow print and are Lawsons.

Mr. Whitney's writing desk has cabriole legs, and his desk chair is a 1725–75 cherry corner chair in green leather. There are letters on his desk blotter, also a plumed pen, pencils, and a letter opener. There is also a silver inkstand (the original by Philip Syng, Jr., made for the Pennsylvania Assembly and given to the Continental Congress in 1775. This inkstand was used at the signing of the Declaration of Independence), a

pair of 1812 brass candlesticks, and a green Chinese scrap basket from Hong Kong.

On the Sheraton stand by an armchair are Mr. Whitney's racing binoculars, a Bible, and Victorian bookends with three books.

The pine knickknack cabinet by the fireplace contains a Dresden plate, a handmade basket, and a china pitcher of Wedding Ring pattern.

The mahogany highboy is a Delaware Valley one (1730–50). On it are a very early China-trade ginger jar and an ironstone pitcher and basin.

There are two original oil paintings by Mrs. Holmes; one is titled "Fall Landscape," and the other is "Seascape." The other oils are two landscapes; one "Summer New England Scene," the other "Autumn New England Scene." There are also a *Fraktur* drawing done in ink by the Pennsylvania Mennonite Germans about 1780, and a clipper-ship print.